W9-CXY-754

495

brief encounters
Edwin Moore

Chambers

CHAMBERS
An imprint of Chambers Harrap Publishers Ltd
7 Hopetoun Crescent
Edinburgh, EH7 4AY

www.chambers.co.uk

First published by Chambers Harrap Publishers Ltd 2007

© Edwin Moore

All rights reserved. No part of this publication may be reproduced,
stored in a retrieval system, or transmitted by any means, electronic,
mechanical, photocopying or otherwise, without the prior permission
of the publisher.

A CIP catalogue record for this book is available from the British Library.

ISBN 978 0550 10350 5

Editor: Liam Rodger
Prepress Controller: Andrew Butterworth
Publishing Manager: Camilla Rockwood

FSC
Mixed Sources
Product group from well-managed
forests and other controlled sources

Cert no. SGS - COC - 2061
www.fsc.org
© 1996 Forest Stewardship Council

Designed and typeset by Chambers Harrap Publishers Ltd, Edinburgh
Printed in Great Britain by Clays Ltd, St Ives plc

CONTENTS

Ancient and Medieval Meetings

Renaissance and Baroque Encounters (16th and 17th centuries)

Enlightenment Encounters (18th century)

Regency and Victorian Encounters (19th century)

From one World War to another (20th century to 1945)

Modern Times
(20th century from 1946)

INTRODUCTION

There have been three broad rules for a meeting to be included in this book: (a) the persons meeting should be well-known; (b) they should meet only once in glancing, ship-in-the-night fashion; (c) the meeting should have some real significance.

In practice, however, I have decided that (a) in a few entries, we can live with the name of one of the participants being not commonly known. For example, Billie Holiday is a well-kent name, though Abel Meeropol is not, but the meeting is well worth including; (b) occasionally the participants are allowed to have met more than once – for example, Tom Cribb and Tom Molineaux fought twice, but it is their bloody 39-round encounter in 1810 that matters, and though the great atheist Robert Ingersoll served under Lew Wallace during the American Civil War, their later chance encounter on a train is too good to omit; (c) the meeting need not be of great significance if it is sufficiently interesting – for example, the delightful encounter in 1900 between the American novelist Winston Churchill and the now rather better-known Winston S Churchill. Also, it should be a given that we are sure that an encounter actually took place, but I am compelled to make one exception: the strange and fascinating LA-wasteland case of L Ron Hubbard and Aleister Crowley. What was all that about? The truth is, I spent too much time researching that alleged encounter to give it up and, to paraphrase the great Neil Innes (late of the Bonzo Dog Doo Dah Band), I suffered to put that entry together and now it's your turn.

Some wonderful encounters didn't get in because, alas, we can say with some certainty that there was no meeting. In these web-reliant days, grizzled oldies will tell you young 'uns to check printed sources. Well, an article in the archive of a prominent Scottish newspaper will inform you that Oscar Wilde once gave Edwin Moore his coat because the man was cold, and being that Edwin Moore myself, I can say with certainty that Oscar Wilde never gave me his coat – and I am not yet into my 13th decade, either. And never mind newspapers: despite what a few biographers will tell you, Marlene Dietrich does not act with Garbo in Pabst's 1926 movie *Joyless Street* – Dietrich was home nursing her child; nor, despite the 1966 movie *Khartoum*, did the Mahdi and General Gordon ever meet (though, improbable as it seems, they corresponded, as one crabby Victorian gentleman to another). And despite Sir Walter Scott, Richard the Lionheart never did meet Saladin, though Saladin once sent him peaches and snow. However, Richard did meet Saladin's brother, and an intriguing meeting it was too. That meeting is in this book, along with 99 others that offer little windows on human history.

The diligent reader will discover that cross referencing could have been more exhaustive. To have added all relevant cross references would have devoured too much space, but you can always play a variant of the Kevin Bacon game, and see how easy it is to make improbable links between people. Nessie, for example (though admittedly not a person) links St Columba (died 597) and Aleister Crowley (died 1947), and James Boswell pops up everywhere among his contemporaries, whether having a fling with Rousseau's mistress in 1766, visiting Flora MacDonald in 1773, or interviewing the Mohawk chief Joseph Brant in 1776.

The space factor means that a lot of desirable but peripheral stuff has had to go. In one entry alone, **1887: Queen Victoria meets Black Elk**, out has gone Buffalo Bill's manager kicking off Glasgow Celtic's worst-ever home defeat (beaten 8-0 by the mighty Dumbarton), Annie Oakley observing that if her aim had been worse – while shooting the ash from a cigarette held in the hand of the future Kaiser Wilhelm – history might have been better; and we've also had to leave out Queen Victoria telling Annie she was 'a very, very clever little girl', and Sitting Bull calling her Watanya Cecilia, 'Miss Sure Shot'.

If you like that sort of thing, you will love this book. Here you will find W E Johns (creator of Biggles) interviewing Lawrence of Arabia for a mechanic's job; a puzzled Persian emperor wondering who these smug Spartans are; Pocahontas being unimpressed by James I; Jackie Kennedy popping downstairs to meet Princess Diana, and much more. As Donald Rumsfeld (who almost got in the book, but was squeezed out by George Bush) would perhaps put it, this is stuff as it happened, and we are all interested in stuff.

Finally, thank you (once more) to my brilliant editor, Liam Rodger, without whose skill and many helpful suggestions this book would have been a horrendous struggle; Alice Goldie and Mike Munro, for their many helpful comments on the text; George MacDonald Fraser, shedder of light into history's odd corners; Maureen of Caledonia Books in Glasgow, for her generous help in finding books for me to scavenge upon; and Merlin Holland for his valuable comments on Oscar Wilde meeting Walt Whitman.

This book is for Helen, Rowan and Joe.

ANCIENT *and* MEDIEVAL MEETINGS

— *1* —

C. 540 BC: CYRUS THE GREAT DOESN'T KNOW WHAT TO MAKE OF THE SPARTAN EMBASSY

In the 540s BC Cyrus the Great, the Persian emperor, was busy expanding his empire. He had conquered the Medes and established control over much of the Near East when a stroke of luck handed him Lydia (roughly the western half of present-day Turkey) on a plate. Lydia's ruler, King Croesus, decided to attack Cyrus in 547 BC after receiving a gloriously ambiguous message from the Delphic oracle saying that if he attacked Cyrus, 'a great empire would be destroyed'. He duly attacked, and discovered that the empire doomed to fall was his own – Cyrus defeated Croesus and absorbed Lydia into the Persian empire.

Lydia had been allied with the warlike Spartans of mainland Greece, who were concerned about the fall of Croesus, and sent an embassy to the Persian emperor in about 540 BC. The encounter was in all likelihood as classic an example of cross-purposes as could be found in Ancient or Modern history. The Spartan embassy was sent both as a mark of reproof and a thinly veiled threat: mess again with Greeks or their allies and you might have to mess with us. But Cyrus seems to have been anything but unnerved by the Spartan emissaries clad in vermillion cloaks and wearing their hair effeminately long and oiled. Evidently baffled, he asked some Greeks at his court 'Who are the Spartans?', but was not much interested in the answer. The Spartans were definitely a weird bunch, but, however warlike, not of concern to the conqueror who would shortly be adding the great city of Babylon to his domains.

The Spartans, for their part, would be unaware on their voyage home that Cyrus had very likely already forgotten their eccentric embassy. For the Spartans, as for all Greeks, Asia was where the great city of Troy had fallen to the Spartan king Menelaus and his cast of Greek heroes, as recorded by Homer in the *Iliad*, the Greeks' epic poem of the Trojan War. The Spartans were, as they saw it, returning from a land they had once subdued in fire and blood, home to a Sparta dominated by the tomb of Menelaus and his troublesome wife, Helen. The idea that Troy's destruction was little thought of (or perhaps even unknown) in the land of Cyrus, was not one that would have been likely to occur to them.

What happened next

Cyrus could safely forget about the Spartans, but not so his successors. The question, 'Who are the Spartans?', arose again at Thermopylae in 480, where an astonished Persian scout watched 300 Spartans comb each other's hair in calm disregard of the massive Persian army which would soon be streaming up the pass towards them. The Persian invader Xerxes offered good terms for surrender of arms: the Spartan leader Leonidas said in return: 'come and get them'.

Also standing with the Spartans in the pass were about 300 of their own serfs (helots), around 400 Thebans, and 700 Thespians ('acting Spartans', perhaps?), but it is those chilling, doomed Spartans who are most remembered in the many accounts of the battle down the centuries. As the historian Tom Holland says: 'shielded behind their mountain frontiers, self-sufficient, xenophobic and suspicious, the Spartans took but never gave, spied but never revealed'.

—2—

336 BC: ALEXANDER MEETS DIOGENES (WHO IS NOT IN THE LEAST IMPRESSED)

Not long before his death at the age of 32 in 323 BC, Alexander the Great is said to have wept that there were no more worlds to conquer. The Cynic philosopher Diogenes, by contrast, believed that nothing was worth making a fuss about, certainly not human vanity and ambition. He was described by Plato as 'Socrates gone mad', in that he took the healthy scepticism advocated by Socrates to extremes and wilfully challenged all authority and custom. When he ate food in the marketplace this was regarded as a bit shocking. How people felt when he defecated and masturbated in public can only be imagined, yet for Diogenes these were (paradoxically perhaps) simply public demonstrations that his appetites were no one's business but his own. Diogenes and Alexander were contemporaries, so it would have been interesting if proponents of such contrasting world views had actually met. In fact, according to the Roman historian Plutarch, they did.

In 336 BC Alexander came to Corinth, the centre of the Hellenic confederacy, where he had serious business in hand. Still aged only 20, he had to bind the fractious Greeks under his leadership and prepare for a military campaign against the mighty Persians. Yet he still took time to search out his favourite philosopher. Diogenes was then in his 70s, and living in a barrel (allegedly on a diet of onions). It's hard to say whether he really was plagued by fetching young women, as depicted in the 1882 painting by John William Waterhouse (one of many depictions over the centuries), but at any rate he was presumably something of a talking point, if not a local tourist attraction.

The meeting between the two has become legendary. Alexander asked Diogenes if there was anything he could do for him, and Diogenes asked him to stop blocking the sun's rays. Alexander's henchmen were taken aback by this disrespect, then astonished when Alexander said that if he were not Alexander he would want to be Diogenes. It was an outcome satisfactory to both parties.

What happened next
Alexander went on to defeat the Persians, and establish an empire stretching from Greece to India, an empire obtained and ruled with ruthless force. The practical request given by Diogenes became Alexander's symbolic image – a young man whose exploits blotted out the sun. Diogenes died in Corinth in the same year as Alexander, 323 BC, indeed supposedly on the same day in June.

Alexander and Diogenes were alike in seeing the world they inhabited as stretching far beyond Greece. Diogenes may have been the first individual to truly think of himself – or at least to declare himself – as a citizen of the world, and Alexander is seen by some as establishing the first world empire, though Cyrus the Great (☛ SEE 1) has a good claim to have got there first.

Neither Cynic philosopher nor conqueror saw different peoples as necessarily barbarians ('barbarian' meaning someone who literally talked rubbish, 'bar bar'). Alexander seems to have thought of the people he conquered – or slaughtered – as being pretty much like his Greek subjects, while Diogenes regarded everyone as equally deluded, wherever they came from.

─3─

327 BC: ALEXANDER MEETS THE NAKED PHILOSOPHERS

In the summer of 327 BC, Alexander the Great was leading his army towards India. The army was bloated with booty, and this hampered progress so much that before reaching the Khyber Pass Alexander destroyed his own loot and that of his friends, and ordered his men to do the same. Alexander took care to burnish his public image, and this was also a way of asserting that his empire was not just about plunder.

After a rebellion against Alexander by a local Indian prince, Plutarch records that he interrogated ten wise men who had apparently encouraged the rebellion. They were obviously regarded by the locals as holy and, disconcertingly, travelled about in the nude. Alexander gave the strange men ten questions to answer, and decreed that a poor answer would mean death. The ten questions and answers became famous (though several sound more like ancient riddles than profound insights). Number three is one of the best known: 'what is the craftiest animal?', with the answer 'the one that has not been found by man yet'. Alexander was impressed with the answers, and rewarded the ten men and gave them their freedom, and asked a tame philosopher in his entourage to find out more. The name given by the Greeks to these wandering holy men was 'gymnosophist', from *gymnos*, naked, and *sophia*, knowledge, but it is not easy to establish just who these 'gymnosophists' actually were. Possibly they were adherents of the Jain religion.

The Greeks were fascinated by the parallels between these holy men and their own traditions. They also favoured nudity among young men, especially at athletic exercises or contests, and they were able to tell the holy men that many Greeks back home held similar beliefs to theirs. Two hundred years previously Pythagoras had taught the transmigration of souls after death, and he had also been a vegetarian (as were other philosophers, such as Diogenes). Pythagoras and the Buddha had been approximate contemporaries, and they were also contemporaries of Zoroaster, Lao-Tzu and Confucius among others. It was a heady age, and naturally people have theorized that ideas had moved from east to west or vice versa, though no one can now trace intellectual indebtedness with any certainty.

What happened next
After an unprecedented mutiny from his men (possibly still sore at having had to destroy their loot), Alexander headed home in 325 BC, but died of fever in Babylon in 323 BC.

The gymnosophist attitude to clothes made a surprising comeback in the late 19th and early 20th century, with a growing interest in naturism in the West. The movement inspired a lot of dippy movies showing naked young Germans throwing beachballs around, but actually seems to have begun among Brits living in India, who in 1891 founded a group called 'the Fellowship for the Naked Trust'. The founder of the Wiccan religion (modern witchcraft), Gerald Gardner, was a prominent member of the 'New Gymnosophist Society', and established a club in the 1920s especially for Wiccan gymnosophists where they could perform their rituals 'sky-clad', a term borrowed from Indian ascetics. Such western interpretations of gymnosophy laid the foundations for the hippy era of the 1960s.

—4—

C. 264 BC: ASHOKA THE GREAT IS CONVERTED TO PACIFISM BY NIGRODHA

Ashoka the Great, who was to be the last Mauryan emperor in India, succeeded to the throne around 270 BC after a protracted and bloody dynastic struggle against rival claimants. Perhaps he did not kill precisely 99 of his 100 brothers, or personally behead 500 enemies (as the legends have it), but the Mauryan empire was clearly a great prize of war, and seemed to many to be worth having a fight over. Ashoka eventually ruled over most of what is now India, Pakistan and Bangladesh, as well as most of Afghanistan and parts of Iran.

The Battle of Kalinga, in which Ashoka crushed a revolt around 264 BC, affected him deeply. According to his own testimony, the fighting cost the lives of over 100,000 Kalinga men, women and children, and 10,000 of his own men. He had inscriptions carved into rocks and onto pillars erected throughout the Mauryan empire proclaiming his edicts and explaining that his remorse had led him to embrace the practice of 'dharma', the way of the Buddha, which counselled compassion to others, and to all life (the significance of the pillars was only rediscovered in the 19th century).

Not long after Kalinga, the already remorseful Ashoka is said to have met the novice Buddhist monk Nigrodha strolling by his palace, who preached to him a sermon on how a good man should live – with compassion and 'heedfulness'. According to the edicts, Ashoka had been studying Buddhism for years, but having met Nigrodha, he now became, in the words of his own inscriptions, a 'lay follower of Buddhism'. Many accounts of this chance meeting between the ruler and the monk fragment into what are symbolic interpretations: we can doubt, for example, that Ashoka literally sent Nigrodha 500 bottles of perfume three times a day for the rest of his life (carried on the backs of elephants).

Whatever the details of the actual meeting and its aftermath, the importance and unique nature of Ashoka's conversion is indisputable. In his edicts (which are the earliest recorded Buddhist writings) we find a monarch addressing his people, telling them he has been a bad man, and that he now wishes to become moral, and to spread his influence through good works rather than evil acts such as war. Capital punishment was abolished, prisoners were to be treated kindly, and laws were passed to protect animals. The empire would co-exist peacefully with its neighbours, and justice would be fair.

What happened next

Buddhism practically died out in India, and only revived under the British in the 19th and 20th centuries. It was British scholars who returned to India the knowledge of its greatest king (Ashoka was not confirmed as the author of the edicts until 1915), and the wheel of Dharma carved on one of his great pillars now appears in the centre of the Indian flag. Thanks to Ashoka, Buddhism spread far and wide in the years of his reign (which ended about 239 BC). He sent missionaries to all the known world (even possibly to Britain), and the religion made a significant impact outside of India, most notably in Sri Lanka, Thailand, and eventually China. H G Wells wrote of Ashoka: 'In the history of the world there have been thousands of kings and emperors who called themselves "their highnesses", "their majesties", and "their exalted majesties" and so on. They shone for a brief moment, and as quickly disappeared. But Ashoka shines and shines brightly like a bright star, even unto this day.'

—5—

52 BC: VERCINGETORIX THE GAUL SURRENDERS TO CAESAR

In 58 BC, long before anyone started muttering about the fateful Ides of March, Julius Caesar was appointed Governor of Transalpine Gaul in what is now southern France. He then began the series of wars which led to the conquest of all Gaullish lands, and which he wrote up in his *Commentaries on the Gallic War* (long a favourite torture implement in grammar school Latin classes). Skilfully exploiting intertribal divisions, Caesar subjugated the Gauls, and even had time to take two whacks at the Britons across the Channel in 56 and 55 BC.

Foreign rule is rarely appreciated, and in Gaul, just as in the Palestine of *The Life of Brian*, better roads and all the other things 'the Romans did for us' never made up for the arrogant governors, the ever-present garrisons of trained killers, the bullying traders with senatorial connections, and, of course, the taxes. The Gaul uprisings began as early as 58 BC, with the final revolt in 52 BC being led by a young nobleman (he may have been only 17) called Vercingetorix. He managed to unite large numbers of Gauls against the Romans, but a hard-pressed Caesar defeated the rebels at the Battle of Alesia. According to popular legend, Vercingetorix surrendered in a theatrical manner, riding into Caesar's camp to kneel at his feet. Illustrations of the great Gaul laying down his sword in front of a suitably impressed Caesar still feature in French schoolbooks. Caesar's own account is altogether more restrained. Vercingetorix tells the leaders of the Gauls (in the words of a Victorian translation) that 'he had undertaken that war, not on account of his own exigencies, but on account of the general freedom' and leaves it to them 'whether they should wish to atone to the Romans by his death, or surrender him alive'. They chose the latter option, and Caesar relates that he 'seated himself at the head of the lines in front of the camp, [and] the Gallic chieftains are brought before him. They surrender Vercingetorix, and lay down their arms'.

What happened next

Caesar does seem to have admired Vercingetorix as a leader of men, and the Romans most definitely admired the fighting qualities of the Gauls. Their independent, martial qualities had been admired for centuries, as is well attested by the famous sculpture of *The Dying Gaul* (itself a Roman copy of a lost Greek original). Vercingetorix was taken to Rome, paraded in front of the mob, jailed, then executed in 46 BC, probably with a garrotte (and possibly not to universal approval in the city). Caesar himself was assassinated two years later.

Despite this brutal end to their story, the more romantic version of their encounter was the one that prevailed. In 1865, Napoleon III had a 20-foot statue of the hero erected at the site of the battle (ancient Alesia was near modern Dijon in eastern France). The statue shows Vercingetorix with a moustache, though contemporary coins show him clean-shaven. Napoleon III was well-whiskered, so perhaps the sculptor wanted to identify his master with the ancient hero.

─6─

AD 385: MAXIMUS EXECUTES PRISCILLIAN FOR HIS BELIEFS

Like the fictional Maximus in the 2000 film *Gladiator*, the 4th-century emperor Maximus was a Spaniard who was popular with his troops. He was one of a series of military commanders who fought for control of the Roman empire in the 4th century and was the first Christian ruler to execute a Christian for his beliefs. His victim was another Spaniard, an ascetic intellectual called Priscillian, described by a contemporary as 'a man of noble birth, of great riches, bold, restless, eloquent, learned through much reading, very ready at debate and discussion'.

Priscillian had many admirers and became a bishop, but he also had many theological enemies. Prompted by the persecution of his followers, Priscillian appealed to Maximus at Trier for imperial protection, but ended up being tried for both sorcery and immorality in a secular court, which was followed by a second trial before Maximus. The encounter was brief and momentous.

St Martin of Tours had been so shocked by the vehemence of the language used against Priscillian that he had also appealed to Maximus not to shed blood, but after Martin left the city Priscillian and several followers were beheaded on the direct orders of

Maximus. They were the first Christians ever to be executed for heresy by fellow Christians. They would not of course be the last …

The executions were quickly condemned by Pope Siricius and by Bishop Ambrose of Milan, and several leading followers of Priscillian, including two bishops, were eventually reconciled to the Church.

What happened next
Maximus, despite his bloodthirsty efforts for the Church, was soon forgotten after being executed by the Eastern emperor Theodosius in AD 388, though his descendants are quite interesting. One presumed great-grandson, Petronius Maximus, was very briefly emperor before being stoned to death in AD 455, and his daughter may have been married to the British king Vortigern, according to the 9th-century inscription on the Pillar of Eliseg in Denbighshire, north Wales.

As with many 'heretics', we know of Priscillian's beliefs primarily from his persecutors (his earliest writings were, astonishingly, rediscovered in 1885). At least some of his beliefs derive from heterodox Manichaean or Gnostic traditions (Gnostics saw the Creation as a flawed, even evil work, rather than the beneficent Creation of a loving God). The most notable ex-Manichaean of the day was Augustine, but there were many Christians who regarded themselves as orthodox, yet sympathized with the inspirational asceticism of men such as Priscillian (and women too: many of Priscillian's followers were women, who were regarded as equals by the men, a feature of many Gnostic groups).

Priscillian continued to be venerated by many Christians in Spain, particularly in Galicia, which was later to be a cause of great concern to Pope Leo I. Priscillian's body was brought back from Trier, and it has been suggested that the human remains discovered at Santiago de Compostela in the 8th century are in fact Priscillian's, and not those of St James. Gnosticism – in the form of Catharism – was to resurface centuries later in Provence, and was suppressed by the Church with great ferocity during the Albigensian Crusade of 1209-55. But by then the world had become accustomed to the spectacle of Christians slaughtering Christians.

~7~

AD 452: POPE LEO I PERSUADES ATTILA THE HUN NOT TO ATTACK ROME

Pope Leo I ('the Great') was renowned for his zeal in bashing heretics – and that's one thing there was no shortage of in the Dark Ages, as hair-splitting theological disputes were a favourite pastime. Leo was especially notable for his campaigns against the followers of Pelagius (a very British heretic, who rejected original sin), and of Priscillian (☞ SEE 6).

In AD 452, however, Leo had to face up to a very pressing temporal matter. Attila the Hun and his forces had been wreaking havoc in northern Italy, and razed at least one city to the ground. Dubbed the 'scourge of God' by the Romans, Attila was undoubtedly a fearsome opponent, though it seems possible that he was not quite the monster he has been portrayed as in European culture. A reliable description of the leader by the Greek historian Priscus portrays a man of moderate tastes: 'In everything... he showed himself temperate; his cup was of wood, while to the guests were given goblets of gold and silver. His dress, too, was quite simple, affecting only to be clean.' Leo was part of an embassy sent, at the request of Rome's feeble emperor Valentinian III, to meet with this Attila the Temperate (whose empire was then the largest in Europe) near Mantua, and plead for an end to the invasion. Attila listened to Leo – and surprisingly withdrew.

The Roman Catholic church has always given the Pope sole credit for Attila's agreement to spare Rome (albeit with the attendance of Saints Peter and Paul, whom Raphael depicts in a 1512 Vatican fresco as hovering menacingly above the meeting). There is no consensus among secular historians as to why Attila left. It seems implausible that Leo could have had any really persuasive arguments to put to a man who had calmly watched as towns and cities were burned at his command. Alaric the Visigoth, who had captured Rome in 410, had died shortly afterwards, and it has been suggested that Attila feared some sort of curse coming upon him if he attacked the city, but fear of more natural horrors such as plague and famine were more likely to have been persuasive factors. More recently, it has been suggested that Rome's Eastern emperor at Constantinople, Marcian, whom historians have traditionally portrayed as holding largely aloof from the trouble in the West, may in fact have posed more problems for Attila than has formerly been thought.

What happened next
For whatever reason, Attila withdrew and died the following year, supposedly (says Priscus) from a nosebleed caused by a wedding night drinking session (he was not much of a drinker, but something about a new wife seems to have caused him to over-indulge). Another account of his death suggests that it was engineered in some way by Marcian. In any case, the Hun empire subsequently collapsed in discord and Attila became a figure of legend in medieval epics. Leo carried on enthusiastically pursuing heretics until his death in AD 461. He is buried in the Vatican, whose power he did so much to consolidate and expand, under an altar specially dedicated to him in St Peter's.

— *8* —

C. 563: ST COLUMBA PREACHES TO BRIDEI, KING OF THE PICTS (AND TELLS NESSIE TO BEHAVE)

St Columba is regarded as perhaps the greatest Irish missionary, but he began his missionary work with a fight over what we now call 'intellectual property rights'. Without permission, he copied a psalm book belonging to the Abbot of Clonard; the subsequent furore led to the Battle of Cooldrevny in 563, in which 3,000 warriors may have died (people took their psalms very seriously in the 6th century ...). Overcome with remorse, Columba left Ireland to preach the gospel to the Picts, and landed on the island of Iona in 563. Iona was a good strategic base for Irish missionaries to heathen Scotland, as it was halfway between the territory of the Scots of Dalriada (who were themselves originally invaders from Ireland) and the great Pictish lands to the east.

Columba travelled to Inverness to meet the Pictish king Bridei. Columba's biographer Adamnan (writing 100 years later) says the missionaries came across Picts burying a man by the River Ness, who had been killed by a monster in the river. Columba then sent one of his obedient followers into the water as bait: the monster duly attacked but quickly fled when Columba ordered it to leave the man alone. This account of a remarkably aggressive Nessie contrasts with her later publicity-shy and peaceful reputation (there have been no other stories of such attacks), so she presumably took good heed of the saint's reprimand. But Adamnan records so many miracles performed by Columba – drawing water from a rock like Moses, multiplying fishes like Jesus, and even driving a demon out of a milk pail – that they all start to seem a bit routine.

Little else is known of Bridei. The Venerable Bede suggests (200 years later) that after his conversion he gifted Iona to Columba. This is not mentioned by Adamnan, who suggests that Bridei was at first hostile to Columba, then got friendly once the obligatory miracle had been performed. In fact, Adamnan does not even claim that Bridei was converted by Columba, and (though it spoils Bede's story) it seems he may well have been a Christian already.

What happened next
Columba died peacefully on Iona in 597. The island would become one of the most important missionary centres in Europe and is now a place of pilgrimage itself. Bridei died around 585, possibly while fighting fellow Picts. By the 10th century, the Pictish kingdoms had been absorbed by the Scots invaders and their strange language forgotten. The Declaration of Arbroath in 1320 would even boast of the genocide of the Picts. By the 19th century, however, the Picts were back in fashion, as can be seen from William Hole's painting (in the Scottish National Portrait Gallery) depicting Columba converting Bridei. As Lloyd Laing points out in his *Celtic Britain* (1979), the work is an anthology of anachronism: Bridei wears a 2nd-century

armlet, an 8th-century brooch, and an 8th-century BC Italian helmet. One of Columba's team carries a 12th-century crozier, while a Pict holds a shield which would have been over 2,000 years old. As Laing says, 'all are set in a rocky scene taken straight from an 18th-century antiquary's druid scrapbook. Yet... there is nothing in this picture that jars on the eye'. The meeting between Bridei and Columba is here firmly set in the world of Celtic myth.

—9—

1050: MACBETH MEETS POPE LEO IX

Thanks to Shakespeare's play of c. 1605, Macbeth is regarded as one of the great villains of history. Shakespeare took his Macbeth from Holinshed's *Chronicles*, which in turn relied on Hector Boece's *Scotorum Historiae* (1527). Boece is a notoriously unreliable source and was writing in any case to bolster the claim of James I to the Scottish throne, while Shakespeare was obliged to flatter his descendant James VI, who became James I of England in 1603.

The character and reign of the real Macbeth was quite different. Macbeth became king after defeating Duncan I in battle in 1040, rather than having him treacherously butchered in his bed by assassins. Duncan may well in fact have been a young warrior rather than Shakespeare's saintly old buffer.

The 11th century was certainly a tough time to be a Scottish monarch, and one of Macbeth's precautions was to take heavily armed Norman knights into his service. It was also a tough time to be a pope, and Leo IX, who became pope in 1049, was himself familiar with Norman power. Norman invaders were causing great strife in Sicily and Southern Italy, and the new Pope did what he could to alleviate the situation.

Macbeth seems to have been a pious chap, and travelled to Rome in 1050, scattering money 'like seed' to the poor, it was said. There is no record of his conversation with Pope Leo IX, so who is to say they did not compare notes on how best to deal with Normans? It is possible that, as the 1913 edition of the *Catholic Encyclopedia* delicately puts it, he 'may be thought to have exposed the needs of his soul to that tender father'. The *Catholic Encyclopedia* is not known for its forthright criticism of the papacy, but even by its own standards the description of Leo IX is highly reverential: in childhood he was 'saintly', and reportedly had trouble reading from a book which turned out to be stolen.

Kingsley Amis portrays the meeting in his fine story 'Affairs of Death'. His Leo IX is a steely character, looking for gifts from his northern visitor. Macbeth is a sad man, haunted by guilt over the blood on his hands, but also keen to tell the pope: 'Scotland is safe and at peace. This has not been customary'. Indeed it was not customary, but Macbeth's rule was popular, and the country lived free from war while he reigned.

What happened next
Leo IX led an army against the Normans in 1053, was defeated, and died a broken man in 1054. His most significant act was his excommunication of the Patriarch of Constantinople in 1054, which caused an un-healable rift between the Catholics and the Orthodox. Macbeth had a good innings for a medieval Scottish king, reigning for 17 years before being killed in battle in 1057 against Duncan's son, Malcolm III. In a development still not really understood, Macbeth's stepson Lulach took the throne. Lulach's father had been killed by Macbeth and it is possible he fought in alliance with Malcolm; in any case, Malcolm ambushed and killed him in 1058. Scottish history at this time begins to resemble a series of *The Sopranos*, with Macbeth's rule as a rare interlude of peace and plenty. Macbeth may be one of the many kings buried on Iona.

～10～

C. 1052: EDWARD THE CONFESSOR MEETS WILLIAM THE BASTARD

Not many medieval kings made it to be saints, with all those unruly barons to bash into line and the many temptations of wealth and power. Anglo-Saxon King Edward, who ruled England from 1042 to 1066, was an exception, and he is now better known as Edward the Confessor (and the builder of Westminster Abbey). He succeeded his unpopular high-taxing half-brother Harthacanute, who is described brusquely in the Anglo-Saxon Chronicle as having 'never accomplished anything kingly'. Edward, according to the Chronicle, was a highly popular successor.

As was the case in Scotland, which also enjoyed an unusual spell of peace in the early 1050s thanks to Macbeth (☛ SEE 9), there were many eyes on the throne. The English throne enjoyed a special prestige: in an era of fast-risen freebooters, men who were often barely a sword's length away from the family cowshed, the English crown shone as the symbol of a dynasty that reached back to the 6th century, almost to the twilight of the Roman Empire, a dynasty which included such heroes as Alfred the Great.

Around 1052, Edward received a visit from William the Bastard, ruler of Normandy. Such historic meetings tend, sadly, to go un-minuted. They may have talked about the weather for all we actually know, but it was one of the most important meetings in English history. Years later – in 1066 – William was to claim that at the meeting Edward had named him his successor. Though the claim may seem farfetched, it is certainly the case that Norman influence was growing in England during Edward's reign. It is often forgotten that there were already Norman settlers in England, and not long before William's visit a group of them was killed in a brawl at Dover. Edward, in an unsaintly gesture, then ordered Earl Godwin to punish the people of the town. Godwin refused to attack his fellow Saxons and was exiled.

Edward's death was enveloped in a fog of claim and counter claim. Godwin's son, Harold of Wessex, claimed that Edward had nominated him on his deathbed, while William got the pope's approval for his version of the 1052 meeting. William also claimed that Harold, while a 'guest' of William's after being shipwrecked in Normandy, had sworn to support the Norman's claim.

What happened next

Edward died in January 1066. William invaded on 28 September, just three days after Harold had destroyed a large Norwegian army led by their giant king Harald Hardrada at Stamford Bridge in the North of England. Harold advanced south, bringing his exhausted forces into battle at Hastings on 14 October. The fight was a close one but ended with Harold's death. William was crowned King of England on Christmas Day. Subsequent English rebellions were brutally crushed, and some historians estimate that over England as a whole, in the period 1066-75, perhaps a fifth of the population died.

~ 11 ~

1192: RICHARD THE LIONHEART MEETS SALADIN'S BROTHER

Since the 18th century, many western intellectuals have portrayed the Crusades as a clash between brutal, uncultured barbarians from the west on the one hand, and a more tolerant Muslim civilization on the other. This is a view that has perhaps led to an over-rosy view of some Muslim rulers, such as the great Kurd Saladin. Saladin's main opponent in legend (and at least partly in history) was of course Richard I of England, the so-called Lionheart. The two were opponents during the Third Crusade of 1189-92, though never actually met despite their wonderfully flowery exchanges in Sir Walter Scott's novel *The Talisman*.

Richard arrived in the Holy Land trailing a reputation for brutality, and reinforced it by killing over 2,700 Muslim hostages in 1191 after the capture of Acre. Saladin, however, liked Richard. During one battle he sent him two horses after his own was killed under him. He also sent him sherbet when he was sick and offered him his personal physician. The two were also linked via the dreaded Shia Assassin sect: Assassins made at least two attempts on Saladin's life, and one of the Assassins who killed Conrad I of Jerusalem claimed Richard had paid for the murder (the case against Richard is unproven).

Richard then proposed – out of the blue – an aristocratic compromise solution to Saladin that would bring about an end to the Crusades: Saladin's brother, Al-Adil, could marry Richard's widowed sister Joanna. Joanna had been Queen of Sicily, and when her husband died, the new king, Tancred, imprisoned her. But when Joanna's scary brother turned up in Sicily in 1190 on his way to Palestine, Tancred released her. Al-Adil and Richard met, but while Joanna loved her brother, she had no intention of marrying a Muslim, nor did Al-Adil want a Christian wife. Al-Adil probably also knew of the widely believed story that Richard and Joanna's mother, Eleanor of Aquitaine, was descended from the Devil. Marriage to a Christian descended from Satan was bad enough; the rumoured ability of a recent ancestor to fly in and out of windows was probably the dealbreaker.

An unenthusiastic Al-Adil reported back to his big brother, who mischievously kept Richard waiting for six weeks before replying that the marriage was a great idea and should take place immediately. Richard, facing outright rebellion from his beloved sister, then asked Saladin if his niece Eleanor would do, and Saladin decided the joke had run its course. Richard and Saladin would never be in-laws.

What happened next
Saladin died in 1193. Al-Adil skilfully brokered peace among Saladin's squabbling nephews, and ended up ruling Egypt and Syria for many years (he also established good relations with the crusader kingdoms in Palestine). Joanna married Raymond VI of Toulouse in 1196, but the marriage was unhappy. Joanna, pregnant with her second child, travelled to seek Richard's protection in 1199, but found him dead of a crossbow wound. Mother and baby died in childbirth. Her surviving son became Raymond VII of Toulouse, who, like his father before him, was forced to take part in the Albigensian Crusade against his Cathar subjects, a war fought with even greater ferocity than the Crusades against the Muslims.

— 12 —

1274: DANTE MEETS BEATRICE

One of the most famous (and briefest) meetings in European literature occurred in Florence when Dante Alighieri met his life's love Beatrice. The meeting is best described in his own words, as translated here by Rossetti: 'I saw her almost at the end of my ninth year [Beatrice was eight]. Her dress, on that day, was of a most noble colour, a subdued and goodly crimson … the secretest chamber of the heart, began to tremble so violently that the least pulses of my body shook therewith; and in trembling it said these words … Here is a deity stronger than I, who, coming, shall rule over me.'

The nine-year-old Dante sounds startlingly precocious, but Dante is not writing a modern autobiography, and is instead exploring the nature of earthly and divine love. The two met again nine years later in 1283 (again in Dante's description as translated by Rossetti): 'passing through a street, she turned her eyes thither where I stood sorely abashed … she saluted me with so virtuous a bearing that I seemed then and there to behold the very limits of blessedness … betaking me to the loneliness of mine own room, I fell to thinking of this most courteous lady, thinking of whom I was overtaken by a pleasant slumber, wherein a marvellous vision was presented to me: for there appeared to be in my room a mist of the colour of fire, within the which I discerned the figure of a lord of terrible aspect … In his arms it seemed to me that a person was sleeping, covered only with a blood-coloured cloth; upon whom looking very attentively, I knew that it was the lady of the salutation who had deigned the day before to salute me. And he who held her held also in his hand a thing that was burning in flames; and he said to me, *Vide cor tuum* ['behold thy heart'].'

Suspicious commentators have noted that Dante seems to have liked things to happen in nines, and as medieval Florence was after all not that big a place, he should surely have seen his beloved Beatrice more than twice in nine years. But as women know, men see what they want to see, and perhaps he was only recording the moments of vision.

What happened next

Dante married a woman called Gemma in 1285, by whom he had four children; Beatrice married a banker in 1287. Asked how he coped with life after her marriage, Dante replied: 'Ladies, the end of my love was indeed the greeting of this lady... in that greeting lay my beatitude, for it was the end of all my desires.' Beatrice died in 1290, aged 24, but reappears in Dante's masterwork, one of the greatest of all poems, the *Divine Comedy* (1308-21), as Dante's guide into Paradise towards 'the Love which moves the sun and the other stars'.

The second meeting between Dante and Beatrice is memorably depicted in that Pre-Raphaelite masterpiece *Dante and Beatrice* (1883), by Henry Holiday. Kitty Lushington, the model for the maidservant in the painting, would later be the inspiration for Virginia Woolf's Clarissa Dalloway – the curious can see what the young Mrs Dalloway looked like by visiting the Walker Art Gallery, in Liverpool, where the painting now hangs.

RENAISSANCE *and* BAROQUE ENCOUNTERS (16th *and* 17th CENTURIES)

━13━

1520: HENRY VIII WRESTLES FRANCIS I

Henry VIII has had a bad press from posterity, largely because he deserves one. One of the few intellectuals to inherit the English throne, he was genuinely interested in all aspects of learning, and corresponded with the humanist Erasmus while still a youth. Although he almost certainly did not compose 'Greensleeves', as used to be believed, he was an accomplished musician and composer.

But from an early age this royal paragon was also fascinated by war. By 1520, England was a growing power in Europe, courted cautiously by the two main forces, the Habsburg emperor Charles V, and Francis I of France (who was also a young ruler flexing his muscles). Though England had a population much smaller than France's, it was managing, as several historians have noted, to punch well above its weight.

Peace was finally made with France, and the two young lions agreed to meet in June 1520 at what is known as the 'Field of the Cloth of Gold', near Calais. It was so called because of the large amount of gold cloth on display, on both costumes and tents. The event lasted a month. The proclaimed intention was to strengthen the bonds between England and France, who were neighbours and should be friends in a rapidly changing world. Two 12-foot paintings – now at Hampton Court – were made to record the meeting, one showing Henry embarking for France, the other showing details of the place and the events.

Cardinal Wolsey, Henry's Lord Chancellor, organized everything. A 300-foot-long palace was built, with 30-foot (mostly cloth) walls; fountains flowed with wine; dozens of priests tended to the gathering's spiritual needs; over 2,000 sheep were eaten; the finest choristers sang; knights jousted ... and Francis and Henry wrestled. The encounter was not planned, and Wolsey would certainly not have wanted it. It was a definite mistake: to have two burly young monarchs wrestling in front of their watchful courts (indeed in front of beady eyes from every court in Europe) was to risk misfortune.

Francis succeeded in pinning Henry to the ground; Henry rose white-faced and furious and the fun was all over.

What happened next

The Field of the Cloth of Gold represents what may well be the biggest outlay in diplomatic expenditure for the least result, effectively a silly and hugely expensive interlude. England and France were back at war within two years, after Wolsey arranged an alliance with Emperor Charles. Henry's soldiers raided France in 1522 and 1523, and he suggested to Charles that they carve up France between them, after Charles captured Francis. Charles was not interested. Pope Clement VII then persuaded Henry into an alliance – the League of Cognac – against Charles, but Henry's war chest was already running out at this point. England was an important player in European affairs, but not one wealthy enough to sustain a European war.

─ 14 ─

1521: MARTIN LUTHER AND FREDERICK THE WISE SEE EACH OTHER AT THE DIET OF WORMS

Around the start of the 1520s, the Portuguese navigator Ferdinand Magellan was passing through the straits which now bear his name, a French king was wrestling with (a young and fit) Henry VIII (☛ SEE 13), and, in 1521, the Germans were having their Diet of Worms. This event has resulted in centuries of giggles among English speakers, as in Hamlet's quip (Shakespeare loved a bad pun) 'Your worm is your only emperor for diet'. The Diet was in fact a general assembly of the numerous princes, dukes and margraves of the Holy Roman Empire, presided over by Emperor Charles V. By this point in history, the empire was, as Voltaire was to describe it, neither holy, nor Roman, nor really an empire, and any such assembly was bound to be fractious.

The main purpose of the Diet was to rein in Martin Luther and the growing Protestant demand for church reformation. In 1520, Pope

Leo X had issued a demand that Luther retract his theses attacking the selling of indulgences, and Luther was called before the assembly to retract the heretical errors in his displayed books. It was Luther's good fortune (or, if you prefer, Providence) that there were other major issues facing the European powers at the time, and present also at the Diet was Luther's temporal lord, the Elector of Saxony, Frederick III, 'Frederick the Wise'. Frederick was the founder of the University of Wittenberg where Luther taught, and, though quite a traditional Catholic (he owned over 19,000 relics, including straw from Jesus's manger), Frederick was becoming increasingly convinced of the need for some measure of reform. He had also obtained a guarantee that Luther would have safe passage to and from the assembly.

The two men did not actually speak to each other, but when Luther was called upon to explain himself, they surely must at least have exchanged looks. Certainly, Frederick would later say that he found Luther 'too bold', and it is entirely possible that Luther sailed closer to the wind than he realized.

Luther probably did not actually say 'Here I stand. I can do no other', but did affirm to the assembly that if his work was not 'from God' then it would perish soon enough. He clearly impressed Frederick, for all his 'boldness'; if he had not, then that would probably have been Luther's last public appearance until brought to the stake.

What happened next
All concerned knew that the guarantee of safe conduct for Luther was pretty flimsy, and when Luther left the assembly he was abducted by a gang of armed men. When the artist Albrecht Dürer (who was to remain a Catholic) heard the news he exclaimed that if Luther was dead there would be no one to explain the gospel. But Luther was not dead. He had been abducted by Frederick's men and spent a year in safety, disguised as a knight (Frederick never visited Luther, possibly fearing a telling off for his beloved relic collection). The rest of the 1520s brought disorder on an unprecedented scale: peasant armies expecting the end of the world ravaged Germany, and in 1527 Rome was sacked by Charles V's ecumenical army of Spanish Catholics and German Lutherans. Charles himself was

horrified by the destruction, but by then it was clear that the old Europe was breaking up in a manner unforeseen at the start of the 1520s.

─ 15 ─

1529: ZWINGLI AND LUTHER ARGUE ABOUT COMMUNION

By 1529, the Protestant Reformation had major strongholds in both Germany and Switzerland, one of the latter centres being Zurich. Most reformers were content with being the power behind the throne (or civil power) but in Zurich the reformer Ulrich Zwingli was effectively both the temporal and spiritual leader: Zurich was a theocracy which predated Calvin's Geneva by almost 20 years. Zwingli's theology was fairly complex in detail, but for contemporaries what really mattered was that he had come independently to the same conclusions about the state of the Church as Luther, and he quickly acquired a large following in Zurich, his influence spreading rapidly to several other Swiss cantons.

There was, however, a bitter difference between Luther and Zwingli over the nature of the Last Supper and the meaning of holy communion: Luther believed Christ was present during communion, whereas Zwingli saw communion as a memorial ceremony. Philip, Landgrave of Hesse – like many Protestant secular leaders – believed it would be a very good thing if the two great reformers could meet and settle their differences, thus establishing a united front of Protestant states against their Catholic opponents.

Philip organized a meeting, which was held at Marburg in 1529. It was a disaster. Luther, as he had shown at Worms (☛ SEE 14), was never a trimmer and was in no mood to compromise his beliefs for the sake of an earthly alliance, especially one forcing him to embrace the views of a 'fanatic', as he called him, like Zwingli. For his part, Zwingli saw Luther as still essentially wedded to Catholic doctrine, a man unwilling to see where his arguments necessarily led. They didn't agree, and didn't like each other (Luther later went so far as to call Zwingli a 'devil'). There was to be no alliance of the disparate German and Swiss Protestant states.

What happened next

The Marburg meeting was a political, spiritual and intellectual failure, but led directly to the drawing up of the Augsburg Confession of 1530 – the primary Lutheran confession of faith – which was presented to the Catholic Emperor Charles V by Luther's much more diplomatic and conciliatory collaborator Philipp Melanchthon (who had in fact prepared the text with Luther's approval). Luther thus did not have to run the risks of another meeting with Charles. In any case, the emperor had far more pressing problems on his plate than doctrinal debates: his own army of Spanish Catholics and German Lutherans had sacked Rome in an orgy of rape and murder in 1527, and the Ottoman Turks had besieged Vienna just a few months previously. In 1531, matters were simplified a bit when Zwingli fell in battle against the Catholic Swiss cantons, and thereafter the future of Protestantism in Switzerland was to lie neither with Zwingli nor Luther, but with the new kid on the theological block, John Calvin.

～16～

1553: CALVIN DISCUSSES THEOLOGY WITH MICHAEL SERVETUS HOURS BEFORE HE IS BURNT FOR HERESY

By 1553, the Protestant Reformation was in full swing and, as Catholics happily pointed out, Protestantism was not a united front: dissidents were everywhere. One of the most famous dissidents of the day was the physician and philosopher Michael Servetus, who in 1553 arrived in Geneva, a city dominated by the reformer John Calvin. Servetus and Calvin may have met before, though some claim Calvin had invited Servetus to a meeting to demonstrate the falsity of his beliefs, but that Servetus failed to show up. They certainly corresponded, and Calvin made plain that their views were incompatible.

Servetus held highly unorthodox views on the godhead and did not believe in the Trinity, which was seriously heretical in both Catholic and (mainstream) Protestant eyes. As Thomas Jefferson said, Servetus simply could not find in Euclid's geometry primer 'the proposition which has demonstrated that three are one, and one is three'. Servetus had been working as a physician in Lyon (where he discovered the pulmonary circulation of blood), and though he had conformed outwardly to Catholic practice, he was denounced to the Inquisition and escaped – the Lyon authorities had to be content with burning him in effigy.

In 1553, while on the run from the Inquisition, Servetus, for reasons that remain inexplicable, arrived in Geneva and went to hear Calvin preach. Possibly he felt that a face-to-face discussion with the fierce reformer would settle their differences. Calvin spotted Servetus in the congregation, which suggests they had met previously. Geneva, however, like all godly places, was a city crawling with spies and informers, and it is likely that a prominent intellectual dissident such as Servetus would have been identified within hours of entering the city. Calvin personally denounced Servetus and arranged for his arrest. He had already said that if Servetus ever came to Geneva he would make sure the heretic died there.

It is very likely that Calvin visited Servetus in his cell on the day of his execution and 'disputed' theology with him. We know that Servetus was badly treated in prison, and was in a terrible condition, so this meeting will have been one of the most cruel and grotesque 'disputations' in history. Calvin is supposed to have asked the city magistrates for beheading rather than burning, but was 'overruled'. Green wood was used for the burning, so that Servetus' agony would be prolonged.

What happened next
The historian Edward Gibbon said 'I am more deeply scandalized at the single execution of Servetus than at the hecatombs which have blazed in the autos-da-fé of Spain and Portugal'. Servetus was burned for two main reasons: Calvin wanted to impress on his rivals in Geneva that he was a hard man with hard remedies, and he also wanted to show Catholics and Protestants everywhere

that Calvinists would not flinch from burning heretics who did not believe in the Trinity. Gibbon believed that personal malice against Servetus was also a factor, and despite the best efforts of Calvin's apologists, then and later, his reputation has never fully recovered from the burning of Servetus. Within weeks of the execution, Protestant intellectuals were expressing their horror at Calvin's act, and in 1554 a historically significant pamphlet was published in Basle arguing against the punishment of 'heretics'.

~17~

1556: JOHN DEE THE MAGICIAN INTERROGATES JOHN PHILPOTT

The magician and scientist John Dee (1527-1609) has long been an object of fascination both to his contemporaries and to posterity. Scholars have attempted to play down his sinister experiments in the occult; after all, even Isaac Newton had his flaky side, spending years of his life on what we now see as eccentric theological speculation. But it is Dee the conjurer who survives in popular tradition (as does the relationship between Dee and his assistant, the medium Edward Kelley, who persuaded Dee that an angel wanted them to share Dee's young wife).

Dee was described by Elizabeth I as 'my philosopher', but this philosopher had an earlier, less well-known and rather horrible career. He had been one of Bishop Bonner's assistants during the reign of Elizabeth's predecessor, the Catholic Mary I, and had practised the dark arts of interrogation on suspected Protestant heretics. Dee himself had gone into Bonner's custody in August 1555 as a suspected heretic, yet quickly, and mysteriously became one of Bonner's chaplains, in which capacity he helped interrogate the cleric John Philpott. Philpott was a clever man, a Latin poet and Hebraist, and while well known for being outspoken, was also popular; altogether an uncommon assortment of traits in any period.

Philpott was taken from his cell to face Bonner and other senior clerics on 19 November 1556. Dee was one of the interrogators. No official account of the questioning survives, but Philpott's own account was smuggled out and has been preserved. He clearly held his own against both Bonner and Dee, and when Dee left the room at one point, Philpott called after him: 'Master Dee, you are too young in divinity to teach men in the matters of my faith. Though you be learned in other things more than I, yet in divinity I have been longer practised than you'. As Dee's biographer Benjamin Wolley points out, this is a fairly clear reference to Dee's reputation as a magician. Rumours about Dee's experiments in the occult were clearly circulating, and Bonner, in response to a letter from Philpott being found on another religious dissident, asked fellow bishops, with the clunking irony of the eternal oppressor, 'is this not an honest man to belie me, and to call my chaplain a great conjuror?'.

On 18 December Philpott was taken to the stake at Smithfield. He recited a few psalms, tipped the executioners, and seems to have died as calmly in the flames as any man possibly could.

What happened next
The period during which Philpott was martyred was one of great significance in British and Reformation history. It is fair to say that not all of the Protestant martyrs were universally attractive or admirable figures – though none deserved their fate – but there were also many, such as Philpott, who were good as well as principled men, willing to endure a truly awful death for what they believed in. Dee, in contrast, went on to become an influential establishment figure during the reign of Elizabeth, a reign that officially celebrated the memory of men such as Philpott, yet allowed shadowy men such as Dee to prosper now that it was the turn of Roman Catholics to be tortured and executed.

~ 18 ~

1593: ELIZABETH I MEETS GRACE O'MALLEY THE PIRATE

'To promote a woman to bear rule, superiority, dominion, or empire above any realm, nation, or city, is repugnant to nature, contumely to God ... the subversion of good order, of all equity and justice' wrote John Knox in 1558. He had of course, Mary, Queen of Scots in mind, but the polemic was badly timed as, in the same year, Protestant Elizabeth ascended the English throne.

Elizabeth and Mary were by no means the only strong women in positions of authority throughout Europe. Grace (or Grainne) O'Malley is described in the *Dictionary of National Biography* as a 'chieftain's wife and pirate'. It is of course the latter job title that attracts the eye, but the wives of clan chiefs and lords were often more than capable of running the family business when the men were posted missing.

The O'Malley family base was in Mayo, in the far west of Ireland. By the time Elizabeth's Lord Deputy, Sir Henry Sidney (who created the Irish county system) visited Grace in 1577 she had already outlived one husband (an O'Flaherty) and was described by Sidney as a 'most famous femynyne sea captain'. Her second husband was a Burke, and Sidney sardonically noted who was the dominant force in the marriage: when they met, O'Malley 'brought with her her husband, for she was as well by sea as by land well more than Mrs Mate with him'. Grace had a fleet of several galleys and several hundred men to sail them. Piracy was undoubtedly part of the O'Malley family income, but the family was hardly unique. Other families had been raiding up and down the west coast of Britain, from as far north as Barra, for centuries. Much of the piratical activity would amount in daily practice to a tax on passing boats, but Grace was clearly not a woman to be trifled with.

Neither, of course, was Elizabeth, as the kings of Europe were learning. The two came together when O'Malley's son Theobald

Burke was arrested under suspicion of rebellious activity. Grace (who had herself been jailed for two years not long before) went to London and pleaded his case with Elizabeth, as one hard-pressed woman to another. The meeting was a great success. Not only was Theobald's release granted, but Grace also pointed out that as a widow she had no claim on her late husband's land under the ancient Irish laws. She asked that Elizabeth grant her this maintenance under English common law, and Elizabeth agreed.

What happened next
Elizabeth's administrators in Ireland dragged their heels in carrying out their orders, so Grace made a quick return visit in 1595 to complain, after which it all went smoothly for her. Our knowledge of her is derived almost entirely from English historical records. Contemporary Irish historians had no interest in her, and many of the stories subsequently told about her in Ireland (and about the meeting with Elizabeth) are clearly much later fantasies. The *DNB* gives Grace's dates as fl. 1577-1597 though she may have outlived Elizabeth, who died in 1603. Her son Theobald, whose pleasing nickname was 'Tibbot of the Ships', fought for Elizabeth against the Spanish at Kinsale in 1599, and became 1st Viscount Mayo in 1627.

~ 19 ~

1605: KING JAMES I INTERROGATES GUY FAWKES

The intention of the conspirators behind the Gunpowder Plot of 1605 was to blow up parliament and create a state of chaos in which Roman Catholics would be restored to power in England. Despite later suggestions that it was a fabrication, the plot was real and, if successful, would have resulted in perhaps the biggest man-made explosion in history to that date. The plot was exposed by the Roman Catholic Lord Monteagle, who was warned off going to parliament by a relative among the conspirators, who were all quickly arrested. Fawkes was arrested in the cellar beneath the House of Lords with a ton of gunpowder at his back.

He was taken to King James' bedchamber at 1 am where he calmly faced down the king and his ministers, saying plainly that he wanted to kill the king and destroy parliament. James asked Fawkes why he was so keen on killing him, and Fawkes replied that the king had been excommunicated by the Pope, and that dangerous diseases required 'desperate remedies'. For good measure, Fawkes told the Scottish king and his courtiers that one of his aims had been to 'blow the Scots back to Scotland', a detail that was suppressed by the government at the time as it could only have encouraged sympathy for Fawkes among the English, many of whom regarded the Scots who accompanied James as a grim lot, extreme both in corruption and in their Protestantism. Robert Cecil, James's right-hand man, described Fawkes at the meeting thus: 'He carrieth himself without any feare or perturbation...; under all this action he is noe more dismayed, nay scarce any more troubled than if he was taken for a poor robbery upon the highway... he is ready to die, and rather wisheth 10,000 deaths, than willingly to accuse his master or any other.'

A thoroughly spooked James then granted permission for torture to be used on Fawkes, instructing the interrogators as follows: 'The gentler tortours are to be first used unto him, *et sic per gradus ad maiora tenditur* ['and thus by steps extended to greater ones'], and so God speed your good work.'

What happened next
The torture Fawkes received on the rack was terrible – we have the signature of his first name 'Guido' after torture and the comparison with earlier samples of his writing is shocking. He was hung, and as the 1911 *Britannica* says, 'the usual barbarities practised upon him after he had been cut down from the gallows were inflicted on a body from which all life had already fled'. As for James, he confirmed his public reputation for cowardice by going into seclusion for a while.

It has been (cautiously) argued that the plot may actually have prevented further anti-Catholic legislation (for fear of provoking other desperate attempts by enraged adherents of Rome), but the lasting effect of the plot was probably to delay Catholic emancipation until the 19th century.

━20━

1617: POCAHONTAS IS UNIMPRESSED BY JAMES I

Hollywood does not always get history wrong, but Disney's cartoon fable *Pocahontas* (1995) certainly takes substantial creative liberties in the interests of engaging contemporary audiences. The film caters both to new stereotypes by portraying the Indians as nature-friendly ecowarriors and to old stereotypes by portraying the English as malignant weeds.

Yet the true story of Pocahontas is more than fascinating enough. 'Pocahontas' may be a nickname meaning 'spoiled child' (her real name was Matoaka) and we know little of her early life. She was the daughter of a Powhatan chief, and it is now generally agreed that John Smith's dramatic story of being saved from execution by Pocahontas in 1607 is not verifiable. The earliest written account of the incident ('she hazarded the beating out of her own brains to save mine') is in a letter from Smith to Queen Anne in 1616, the year that Pocahontas and her husband John Rolfe arrived in London (Pocahontas and Smith were probably never lovers, and they most certainly never married each other).

The trip was a great social success. A Dutch artist engraved a portrait of Pocahontas, the inscription of which describes her as Matoaka, alias Rebecca (her Christian name), and as the daughter of a powerful prince. She was clearly regarded as a high personage by London society. She was received at Whitehall by Queen Anne, and the Bishop of London had the Rolfes to dinner at Lambeth Palace. Samuel Purchas noted that the Bishop 'entertained her with festival state and pomp beyond what I have seen in his great hospitalitie afforded to other ladies'.

She was introduced to King James at a Ben Jonson masque, at which she had a seat appropriate to her royal status. Pocahontas and her party were taken aback to be told they had just been introduced to the king. Pocahontas was surprised that such an unprepossessing individual could be king of England, an opinion, to be fair, that was shared by many of the English themselves (☞ SEE ALSO 19). At least everyone seems to have been reasonably sober on this occasion. At another royal masque three of Queen Anne's ladies were too drunk to stand and another spilled custard on the king.

Tomocomo, a Powhatan priest accompanying Pocahontas, confirmed to John Smith that King James was not quite up to the mark with this splendidly peevish comment: 'You gave Powhatan a white dog, which Powhatan fed as himself, but your King gave me nothing, and I am better than your white dog.'

What happened next
Pocahontas lamented to John Smith that: 'your countrymen ... lie much'. She may have been the first colonial subject to make this comment in English, but not the last. In 1617 she and Rolfe headed for home, but she died on board the ship, and is buried in St George's Church, Gravesend. Her last words were that 'all must die', and she was content that her 'childe liveth'. Their descendants were known as the 'red Rolfes' (George Bush is not one of them as is often asserted, though he does have some family ties with her descendants).

～21～

1653: GEORGE FOX REDUCES OLIVER CROMWELL TO TEARS

George Fox, the founder of the Society of Friends, was born in 1624 in Fenny Drayton, Leicestershire, the son of a weaver. Apprenticed to a livestock dealer, he acquired, he tells us, a reputation for fair dealing: 'A good deal went through my hands ... People had generally a love to me for my innocency and honesty.' In 1643, 'at the command of God', Fox 'left my relations and broke off all familiarity or fellowship with old or young.' There followed several years of wandering and seeking spiritual counsel (the advice received from one priest was to take up smoking).

Fox began to receive internal revelations from God (what he called 'openings'), such as hearing a voice which said: 'There is one, even Christ Jesus, that can speak to thy condition.' On hearing such messages Fox said 'my heart did leap for joy'. The age was not a tolerant one, and even those who themselves dissented from the official church found an individualist and pacifist like Fox too extreme. He was imprisoned many times for expressing his views forthrightly in the street or in church, but his force of character was such that even those who jailed him (including the Sheriff of Nottingham) were often sympathetic.

In 1652, several of Fox's followers formed the nucleus of the so-called 'Quaker' movement in Preston. In 1653, Fox was arrested and taken to meet England's ruler, the Lord Protector Oliver Cromwell, whose reputation for god-fearing piety was matched by one for ruthlessness. The 1650s were rife with religious and political groups, and many charismatic preachers were on the streets with agendas ranging from the restoration of the monarchy to the abolition of private property. Fox was attracting large crowds wherever he went. Cromwell was possibly more curious than suspicious, and the meeting was quite an emotional one. Fox confirmed the peaceful nature of his movement, and asked Cromwell to listen to the voice of God. Fox recorded that the supposedly fearsome Cromwell grasped his hand, and tearfully said: 'Come again to my house; for if thou and I were but an hour of a day together, we should be nearer one to the other.' Cromwell, Fox reported, said he 'wished me no more ill than he did to his own soul. I told him if he did he wronged his own soul; and admonished him to hearken to God's voice, that he might stand in his counsel, and obey it; and if he did so, that would keep him from hardness of heart; but if he did not hear God's voice, his heart would be hardened. He said it was true.'

What happened next
The possibility that Cromwell could have become a Quaker was never very likely. Though this was an age of dramatic conversions, there were no more tears on Cromwell's part when they met again in 1656. Fox was seeking toleration for his persecuted Quakers, and urged Cromwell not to think of the crown but to lay down his

worldly power at the feet of the Lord. It was clearly another meeting of mutual liking, but not one of minds. They met again just before Cromwell died, in 1658. Fox wrote that the Protector looked like a 'dead man'.

~22~
1671: COLONEL BLOOD MEETS KING CHARLES II IN THE TOWER

Colonel Thomas Blood, it has been said, lived a life with 'few parallels'. He was born around 1617, in Meath, say some sources, but he is also claimed by County Clare. Blood did military service in Ireland and England during the Civil War, although which side he fought on, and for how long, remains unclear. His 'colonelcy' may have been self-awarded. By 1651 he had a Lancashire wife (and six children) and lands in both England and Ireland. He spent most of the 1650s in Ireland, and was regarded as a good Protestant landowner and Cromwellian loyalist.

The Restoration of 1660 saw many of Cromwell's supporters lose assets to triumphant Royalists, and by 1662 Blood was involved with other malcontents in a botched plot to capture Dublin Castle. The plot was structured like an Ealing comedy (it would make a great movie) and involved the throwing of loaves of bread at the guards to distract them. Blood escaped to England, where he associated with fellow nonconformists and conspirators. He was attached to the Fifth Monarchy movement, which believed Jesus was returning to rule mankind soon, a belief Blood sincerely shared – indeed it was one of the few certainties about the man's beliefs. In 1667 he rescued a friend being escorted to prison, killed several troopers, and then hid out for a few quiet years, practising as a physician in Kent.

In 1670 he abducted the Duke of Ormonde in St James's Street. Blood's harebrained intention was apparently to hang Ormonde from the public gallows at Tyburn. Ormonde escaped, and his son publicly accused the Duke of Buckingham, a protector of nonconformists, of hiring Blood to kill his father. The following year saw Blood's most famous exploit, one of the most audacious thefts in history. Disguised as a clergyman, he was flukily caught leaving the Tower of London with the Crown Jewels. Blood was imprisoned – in the Tower – and refused to speak with anyone but the king. Charles II went to see him, and after the meeting, to general amazement, the remarkable Colonel emerged from the Tower with a pardon – and a pension.

What happened next
Exactly what Blood said to Charles is unknown, unfortunately, but it must have been persuasive. Certainly, Blood was by now privy to many dark secrets of both state and dissident groups. In 1672 the government was to issue a 'declaration of indulgence' for nonconformists, who were everywhere and a great nuisance, especially with a war with the Dutch looming. Charles may have been the 'merry monarch', but he was certainly nobody's fool and evidently decided that a live Blood was of more use to him than a dead one. Blood died in 1680 aged 62, probably of natural causes. He was dug up again soon after burial, by someone who presumably knew his previous slippery record, and wanted to make sure it really was his body in the grave.

~23~

1675: AURANGZEB EXECUTES THE SIKH GURU TEGH BAHADUR

Born in 1618, Aurangzeb ascended to the Mughal throne of India in 1658, with what has been described as 'feigned reluctance'. How reluctant he actually was can be judged from the fact that he defeated his brothers in a succession struggle, and kept his father, the fifth Mughal (Shah Jehan, who built the Taj Mahal) confined until he died in 1666.

Aurangzeb is a hero to many Sunni Muslims, who regard him as a strong ruler who was preceded and followed by weak ones. He certainly did not seek much in the way of accommodation with his Hindu subjects, but instead encouraged conversion to Islam and had no qualms about destroying Hindu temples. He also didn't think much of Muslims who differed from the views he espoused, and when he captured Hyderabad in 1687 he stabled his horses in the Shia mosques.

Hence, an encounter between Aurangzeb and Guru Tegh Bahadur, the ninth of Sikhism's ten gurus, was never going to be a meeting of like-minded individuals. Tegh Bahadur had received both religious and martial training in childhood, but after several years of fighting the Mughals, in 1656 he chose the contemplative life and spent several years in retreat, and then in missionary work. News of Muslims converting to Sikhism as a result of Tegh Bahadur's influence infuriated Aurangzeb, who in 1675 had the Sikh guru brought to Delhi in chains.

The interrogation of Tegh Bahadur by Aurangzeb was brutal. He challenged the guru to perform a miracle to prove he was a prophet of God, and when Tegh Bahadur refused, saying that he was not a conjuror but a man of God, Aurangzeb told him that if he did not convert he would be tortured to death. Tegh Bahadur insisted in return that there could be no compulsion in religion – itself an Islamic precept – and defended the right of the individual to choose which religion to follow. Kept in an iron cage and starved, Tegh Bahadur was forced to watch as his friends were savagely tortured and killed, before he himself was publicly beheaded.

What happened next
Tegh Bahadur's martyrdom is unusual in the history of religion in that he died not just for Sikhism but for the rights of others to practise their religion. The butchering of the ninth guru earned Aurangzeb the undying hatred of Sikhs across the North Indian plain, and it was to be a costly hatred. Aurangzeb ruled for 46 years, but spent the last 26 years of them constantly at war with Hindus and Sikhs, until his death in 1707. As Bamber Gascoigne says in *The Great Moghuls* (1971), the 16th-century Mughal ruler Akbar, who sought reconciliation between all religions (and became a vegetarian late in life) had 'disrupted the Muslim community by recognizing that India was not a Muslim country. Aurangzeb disrupted India by behaving as if it were'.

ENLIGHTENMENT
ENCOUNTERS
(18th CENTURY)

―24―

1746: BONNIE PRINCE CHARLIE MEETS LORD LOVAT AFTER CULLODEN

The second Jacobite uprising began in 1745 when the Young Pretender Charles Edward Stuart – Bonnie Prince Charlie – landed in the Hebrides to raise the clans in rebellion against George II. One of the Highland lords that Charlie wanted to be sure was onside was Simon Fraser, Lord Lovat. Fraser, otherwise known as 'the Fox', was possibly the most untrustworthy man in Scotland. He became the 11th Lord Lovat in 1733 after decades of villainy, including kidnapping and forcing a marriage (later annulled) on his cousin. He had converted to Catholicism before the first Jacobite Rising in 1715, in which he skilfully avoided taking sides until it was clear the Jacobites would lose, after which he helped himself to their lands.

In 1739, Lovat had promised his support to Charlie if the French would join in, but when French ships were spotted off the Firth of Forth, he instead took to his bed. After the Jacobite victory at Prestonpans, the old rogue at last mustered men for Charlie, but told loyalists it was all his son's doing. Several reference sources still assert that Lovat was present when the Jacobites were finally beaten at Culloden, but this was not so. His own judgement on the battle cannot be improved upon: 'None but a mad fool would have fought that day.'

Charlie and Lovat finally met as the Prince retreated, on the night after the battle, when Lovat took him into one of his houses on Loch Mhor for a fast-food dinner and some fatherly advice. Lovat recommended the 'try again until you succeed' example of Bruce and the spider to the Prince. Charlie's response is not recorded, but none was needed. Both men were well aware that the rising had been a close-run thing, and that if Lovat had put his weight behind the campaign it might have succeeded. Long presented in popular mythology as an England-Scotland game, the 'Forty-Five' was a more complex affair. For many Scottish Protestants, the rising brought the threat of Catholic domination, while many English

Tories still regarded the Hanoverians as German usurpers. But the game was clearly up for both the young prince and the old 'Fox'. Charlie fled and eventually escaped to France, while Lovat, realizing that even he could not scheme his way out of this one, also fled and was caught hiding in a hollow tree on an island in Loch Morar.

What happened next
The great artist William Hogarth was an old acquaintance of Lovat (who was as equally at home in London as in Inverness), and drew a much-admired portrait of Lovat while he stopped at St Albans on his way to the Tower of London. It catches the charm and menace of the man, and sold over 10,000 copies at a shilling each.

Found guilty by his peers, after a trial in which he conducted his own defence with lordly panache, his closing words were: 'I wish you an eternal farewell. We shall not meet again in the same place; I am sure of that.' In 1747 the 80-year-old rebel became the last man to be publicly beheaded in Britain. His death was preceded by those of several spectators who were crushed when a stand collapsed. The no-longer Bonnie Prince Charlie died 41 years later aged 68.

— 25 —

1746: FLORA MACDONALD HELPS BONNIE PRINCE CHARLIE ESCAPE

The tale of how Flora MacDonald helped rescue Bonnie Prince Charlie after the collapse of the Jacobite Rising has often been told in books and movies, and is one of those rare stories in which little is gained by embellishment. Flora has sometimes been portrayed as a poor Jacobite lass, running barefoot through the heather. In fact she was related to the main MacDonald chiefs, was connected to the all-powerful Campbells, and could play the spinet as well as any other well-bred young gentlewoman of her time. She was also Presbyterian, not Catholic, and contrary to legend was in no way an enthusiastic Jacobite.

Charlie's flight westwards after the defeat at Culloden had brought him to South Uist, where he found temporary refuge among some of Flora's relations. Flora arrived in South Uist on family business and opened the door one day to find one of her kinsmen standing there equipped with a prince and a plan: here was Bonnie Prince Charlie, and he would be taken to safety disguised as Flora's maid.

Accounts of the meeting differ in detail, but it seems clear that it was a personal plea for her help from Charlie that swayed Flora. She agreed to help out of charity, and later told King George's favourite son, Prince Frederick, that she would have helped him in just the same fashion. Charlie and Flora certainly hit it off. He wanted to hide a pair of pistols in his petticoat and when Flora pointed out that this would cause problems if he was searched, he replied: 'If we shall happen to meet with any that will go so narrowly to work in searching as what you mean, they will certainly discover me at any rate.'

Flora's stepfather, a tough character called One-Eyed Hugh, was a militia captain in command of the Benbecula-South Uist crossing, and he let his stepdaughter and her odd companion, whom he described as 'one Bettie Burke, an Irish girl, who, she tells me, is a good spinster', travel to Skye. Hugh was quite probably sympathetic to the Jacobites, and we can assume he knew exactly who 'Bettie Burke' was, and that he saw his action as a calculated risk that might pay off in the end in some way.

Charlie escaped in a French ship and Flora was taken prisoner, but treated well. Curiously, the Highland oral traditions have little to say about Flora: as the *Dictionary of National Biography* says, 'even Lady Nairne failed to use such obvious material for a pro-Jacobite song'. Grace O'Malley was similarly ignored in Ireland (☞ SEE 18), and we only know these Celtic heroines from English testimony. Certainly from July 1747 (when Flora was released and given £1,500 raised for her in London) her reputation as a heroine to just about everyone in Britain was secure.

What happened next
Flora married a kinsman, a farmer called Allan MacDonald, commonly described as a personable chap, but not much of a businessman, who had a farm at Flodigarry on Skye. They had seven children between 1751 and 1766, and were visited by Dr Johnson and Boswell.

SEE *1773: Johnson and Boswell visit Flora MacDonald*.

~26~

1747: J S BACH MEETS FREDERICK THE GREAT

The meeting in Potsdam, in 1747, between the 62-year-old composer and organist, Johann Sebastian Bach, and the 35-year-old King Frederick II of Prussia (known also as 'the Great'), has not figured largely in biographies of Frederick the Great (in one major work it is briefly skated over in a footnote). Other writers, such as Joseph Baines in his *Evening in the Palace of Reason* (2005), see the meeting as hugely significant, an encounter between the new age of Reason and an older age of Faith.

Frederick employed Bach's son, Carl, as a court musician. The son was the future of music, the servant of an enlightened despot who believed in the distant, non-intervening god of Enlightenment philosophy – or Deism – rather than the loving and chastising god of traditional Christianity. The father was the past of music, a church organist who belonged firmly to a receding age which still believed in a deity who took an interest in humanity, and was adored in turn by His creation. It was the son's duty to write music that would appeal to his employer, but the father saw his duty as writing music that would appeal to his God.

When Frederick heard 'Old Bach' was visiting Carl he invited the master to hear him play a theme on the pianoforte. Pianos were still a rarity, and a great status symbol, and Frederick presumably wanted to show the old-timer his fancy new instrument, as well as display his musical skills. The king invited Bach to make – there and then – a three-part fugue from the theme he had played. Bach completed the task so well that Frederick asked him to turn the 'Royal Theme' into a six-part fugue. The 20th-century composer Schoenberg saw this as a spiteful request on Frederick's part, an almost impossible request designed to embarrass the old master of the unfashionable art of counterpoint.

What happened next
The work produced by Bach (in a fortnight!) in response to Frederick's test was *The Musical Offering*, a high point in western music, a work of great beauty and also one that contains many teasing intellectual riddles. We don't know what Frederick thought of the work. Probably not much, if indeed he ever played it, and he was off to war again soon anyway. Bach's music slipped into an obscurity from which it was dramatically rescued when Mendelssohn conducted a performance of the *St Matthew Passion* in 1829 (he observed that it had been left to a Jew to restore the greatest piece of Christian music). From that point on, Bach has been seen as one of the greatest composers of all time, while Frederick is largely remembered as the creator of Prussian militarism (though to be fair, he made some progressive changes, such as abolishing torture).

—27—

1752: CASANOVA MEETS MADAME DE POMPADOUR (AND MAKES SOME AWFUL JOKES)

Chapter VII of Casanova's memoirs begins with the beguiling heading 'My Blunders in the French language'. It is of course an eternal requirement of foreign wits visiting Paris to bear witness to how inferior Parisians make even sophisticates feel.

Casanova – who had a knack of getting to know everybody who mattered – had got himself invited to see an Italian opera at Fontainebleau, where he would be able to hobnob with the court, and found himself sitting under Madame de Pompadour's box.

Pompadour was a former courtesan and lover of Louis XV, so was one of the most influential people in France. Casanova was a womanizer, a spy, a freemason and a magician (he was to be imprisoned for witchcraft in 1755 in Venice), so he was not just a sycophant; Casanova really *needed* friends in high places.

One of the opera singers sang a bit shrilly, and Casanova snorted with laughter, as a Venetian opera buff would. One of Pompadour's companions (dressed as a knight of the Order of the Holy Ghost) sardonically enquired of Casanova what country he came from, to which Casanova replied 'Venice'. The knight then said he himself had laughed in Venice during operas, to which Casanova replied that no one would have objected. Perhaps this was not the wittiest of exchanges, but it amused Pompadour (maybe, as they say, 'you had to be there'). She asked Casanova if he was indeed from Venice 'down there': Casanova replied that Venice was 'up' in relation to Paris, and there followed much jolly banter in the courtly box as to whether Venice was up or down in relation to Paris. Casanova was right, the court graciously concluded.

Casanova was careful not to laugh any more, but blew his nose 'often', again attracting the attention of the knight, who turned out to be Marshal Richelieu (grand-nephew of the mighty cardinal). Richelieu suggested that a window might be open, and Casanova – by now struggling a bit in this epic contest of repartee – mispronounced a French word in reply, and the court fell about laughing, in the traditional French response to foreigners' mispronunciations. Casanova made a quick recovery with an off-colour quip about an actress's legs, which included (he honestly records) an unintentional but fitting pun, thus establishing him as a formidable wit. He became a popular figure about town, and, as he proudly said, his 'jeu de mots' became 'celebrated'. Such were the joys of the *Ancien Régime*, soon to be brought to an end by the French Revolution.

What happened next
Casanova and Pompadour bumped into each other later, in 1757, after Casanova returned to Paris having escaped from prison in Venice. Casanova records that the 'fair marquise' asked how his

exile was and hoped that he would stay in France, indeed would help him stay. Casanova stammered his gratitude. At this time he was busy with various madcap schemes, including inventing the state lottery, and eventually fled France in 1760 to escape his debtors. He may also have written part of the libretto for Mozart's *Don Juan* in 1787, and developed a taste for dressing up in women's clothes (his great and only love, Henriette, was also very likely a spy and liked to dress up as a man).

～28～

1764: BOSWELL CALLS ON VOLTAIRE, AND GETS HIM OUT OF BED

James Boswell is now best remembered for his remarkable biography of Dr Johnson, and for his licentious (and long-suppressed) memoirs. In his own day, however, Boswell was one of Europe's prime gossips and a serial visitor to famous personages (he usually introduced himself to foreigners as 'a Scot of ancient family').

A few months after his famous May 1763 encounter with Johnson, in which Boswell demonstrated his formidable talent for absorbing insult, the young Scot set off to tour Europe (for two and a half years), and in December 1764 visited first Rousseau and then Voltaire. At this point 68 years old and one of the acknowledged sages of Europe, Voltaire was used to receiving visitors at his estate of Ferney, on the Swiss border, and he seems to have been both amused and exasperated by this curious (in all senses) visitor, who had made him get out of bed. Said Boswell: 'He was not in spirits, nor I neither.'

They talked of Scotland, and agreed the Scots were not painters. Said the sage: 'To paint well it is necessary to have warm feet. It's hard to paint when your feet are cold.' They talked of Dr Johnson, and the imperturbable Boswell told Voltaire that he planned to visit the Hebrides with Dr Johnson: 'I mentioned our design to Voltaire. He looked at me as if I had talked of going to the North Pole, and said, "You do not insist on my accompanying you?" "No, sir." "Then I am very willing you should go".'

As a devout Christian, Johnson loathed Voltaire's Deist views. Voltaire, in return, says Boswell, had described Johnson, 'affecting the English mode of expression', as a 'superstitious dog'. Boswell, anxious to reconcile the two great men, passed on Johnson's observation that Frederick the Great 'writes just as you may suppose Voltaire's foot-boy to do'. Voltaire (who had issues with his former patron Frederick) was delighted with this comment and described Johnson as 'an honest fellow!'. For all their differences, Johnson's novel *Rasselas* and Voltaire's novel *Candide* are certainly similar in their view of human folly.

By this point, Boswell's charm had obviously won over Voltaire, and he was invited to stay the night. The next day they had an emotional exchange over God and the afterlife, with Voltaire saying: 'I suffer much. But I suffer with patience and resignation; not as a Christian – but as a man.'

What happened next
Discovering news of his mother's death in a Paris newspaper, Boswell returned to Britain in 1766, bringing with him Rousseau's mistress, Thérèse Le Vasseur, to reunite her with Rousseau, then living in England. Boswell and Thérèse had an 'affair' on the trip home. It consisted of 13 acts of sex, after which Thérèse – records Boswell with a total lack of embarrassment – told him he was useless in bed and offered him lessons. Boswell dropped her off at David Hume's, then the next day took her to Rousseau. Voltaire and Rousseau didn't care for each other in life but were united in death, both eventually being buried in the Pantheon.

☛ SEE ALSO *29) 1766: Erasmus Darwin entices Rousseau with a flower*; *30) 1773: Johnson and Boswell visit Flora MacDonald*.

~29~

1766: ERASMUS DARWIN ENTICES ROUSSEAU WITH A FLOWER

In 1762 the French government ordered the burning of Rousseau's educational treatise-novel *Émile*. It argued that children could grow up without vice if they were protected from the evils man had created. This was clearly seditious, and Rousseau fled to Berne, and when the Swiss banished him, he landed in England in 1766.

His English exile had been encouraged and facilitated by the philosopher David Hume, who asked friends at court to get Rousseau a royal pension and also persuaded a friend to give him an empty mansion, Wootton Hall in Staffordshire, to live in.

Despite this support, Rousseau was not the happiest of philosophers at the time, as he had begun to suspect that the English (led by the Scot Hume) were laughing at him. This paranoia led him to write to an astonished Hume saying: 'You brought me to England, apparently to procure a refuge for me, and in reality to dishonour me.'

The physician/philosopher Erasmus Darwin desperately wanted to meet Rousseau, but realizing that a formal introduction would be tricky, came up with a highly engaging ploy instead. Knowing that Rousseau liked to sit in a terraced cave by the mansion, engaged in his now customary melancholic brooding, Darwin sauntered up to the cave one morning and began examining a flower at the cave mouth. After a while, a curious Rousseau emerged from the darkness, and the two chatted amiably about botany, which was, like education, a shared obsession. Darwin was extremely interested in the sex life of plants, and indeed wrote a poem about the subject, 'The Love of the Plants', and he may well have shared his thoughts on the subject with Rousseau.

The meeting was short, but Darwin had done what no other Brit at this time seems to have managed, and established a friendly relationship – continued through letters – with Rousseau. The correspondence has, sadly, been lost. Rousseau's cultural influence is undisputed, but Darwin's achievements have only recently been widely acknowledged, as interest has grown in the Birmingham-based Lunar Society (which he co-founded), a group of Midlands polymaths, who had an immense effect on British intellectual life and culture, from industrialization to the abolition of slavery.

What happened next
Rousseau returned incognito to France the following year, married his mistress (☞ SEE 28) and continued to influence and infuriate his contemporaries. Inspired by Rousseau, Darwin built a small botanic garden (almost the only thing Rousseau liked about England were the gardens) that was praised by Anna Seward thus: 'not only with trees of various growth did he adorn the borders of the fountain, the brook and the lakes, but with various classes of plants, uniting the Linnaean science with the charm of landscape'.

He was of course the grandfather of Charles Darwin and himself an intuitive believer in evolution. He added *E conchis omnia* ('Everything from shells') to the family coat of arms, but was forced to remove it by the Church. He expressed his belief in evolution in his verse: 'imperious man, who rules the bestial crowd ... Arose from rudiments of form and sense, /An embryon point or microscopic ens!' His grandson argued the case rather better – and in prose.

━ *30* ━
1773: JOHNSON AND BOSWELL VISIT FLORA MACDONALD

Lauded throughout the English-speaking world as a heroine (☞ SEE 25), Flora MacDonald found life as the wife of a not very competent farmer to be a struggle, particularly with seven children to bring up.

In 1773, Flora and her husband were visited by the great English writer Dr Johnson, who was on his tour of the Hebrides (for a Gallic, as opposed to Gaelic, view of this trip, ☞ SEE 28). Being a staunch Tory with Jacobite sympathies, Johnson was predisposed to adore Flora, and indeed it was rumoured that in 1745-46 Johnson had taken part in the Jacobite Rising in some way (it is not likely that he did). Boswell and Johnson arrived at the Kingsburgh house of Allan and Flora, where Flora welcomed them: Boswell admired Allan ('a gallant highlander') and was captivated by the 51-year-old Flora, as most men were: 'Here appeared the lady of the house, the celebrated Miss Flora MacDonald. She is a little woman, of a genteel appearance, and uncommonly mild and well bred. To see Dr Samuel Johnson, the great champion of the English Tories, salute Miss Flora MacDonald in the isle of Sky [*sic*], was a striking sight; for though somewhat congenial in their notions, it was very improbable they should meet here.' With great charm, she told Johnson (then in his mid-sixties) that she had heard that Boswell was travelling to Skye, and had 'a young English buck with him'.

Johnson was accorded the honour of sleeping in the bed Bonnie Prince Charlie had slept in the night he stayed at Kingsburgh in 1746. Boswell noted: 'To see Dr Samuel Johnson lying in that bed, in the isle of Sky, in the house of Miss Flora MacDonald, struck me with such a group of ideas as it is not easy for words to describe, as they passed through the mind. He smiled and said, "I have had no ambitious thoughts in it".'

What happened next
In 1774, Flora and Allan emigrated to North Carolina, and when the American War of Independence broke out they raised Highlanders to fight for George III. Both Allan and Flora, like most Loyalists, suffered much hardship after the rebels won, and they returned to Skye, where Flora died in 1790, aged 68. Dr Johnson said of her that her name 'will be mentioned in history, and if courage and fidelity be virtues, mentioned with honour'.

～31～

1774: EDMUND BURKE IS ENRAPTURED BY MARIE-ANTOINETTE

There has never been a solid historical consensus as to whether the great Anglo-Irish statesman Edmund Burke should be regarded as a radical or a conservative, and his own contemporaries often couldn't decide either. Whatever his politics, he was certainly a romantic. His description, in *Reflections on the Revolution in France* (1790), of encountering the 19-year-old Marie-Antoinette in the glorious flesh (he had visited France in 1773) gives eloquent proof of this:

'It is now sixteen or seventeen years since I saw the queen of France, then the dauphiness, at Versailles; and surely never lighted on this orb, which she hardly seemed to touch, a more delightful vision. I saw her just above the horizon, decorating and cheering the elevated sphere she just began to move in, – glittering like the morning-star, full of life, and splendour, and joy...' The queen's fall from power hit the starry-eyed Burke hard: 'little did I dream that I should have lived to see such disasters fallen upon her in a nation of gallant men, in a nation of men of honour, and of cavaliers. I thought ten thousand swords must have leaped from their scabbards to avenge even a look that threatened her with insult. But the age of chivalry is gone. That of sophisters, economists, and calculators, has succeeded; and the glory of Europe is extinguished for ever. Never, never more shall we behold that generous loyalty to rank and sex, that proud submission, that dignified obedience, that subordination of the heart, which kept alive, even in servitude itself, the spirit of an exalted freedom...'

Burke was clearly utterly smitten, and his contemporaries seized upon this extract to have a go at him; an admirer of Burke's called it simple 'foppery', and Tom Paine, in his response to Burke's reflections, *The Rights of Man* (1791), noted with calm disdain that Burke 'pities the plumage, but forgets the dying bird'.

What happened next

Burke was writing a few years before Marie-Antoinette's execution in 1793, when she died bravely. Her husband had been guillotined in January, and she had suffered much in jail; even her 8-year-old son had been taken from her (he would die in 1795) and she said that she had come to realize that suffering is what makes you what you are. She went to the scaffold in October, apologizing for stepping on the executioner's foot. And she never, at any point in her life, said 'let them eat cake' when told the poor had no bread.

~ 32 ~

1774: JOSEPH PRIESTLEY DISCUSSES OXYGEN WITH ANTOINE LAVOISIER (BUT NOT AS WE KNOW IT)

Joseph Priestley was born in 1733 in Leeds to a strongly nonconformist family. By 20 he could read many languages, including Hebrew and Arabic, and in 1755 became a minister. Though brought up a Calvinist, like many nonconformists of his time he gradually abandoned that stark doctrine. His studies in electricity (encouraged by Benjamin Franklin, who became a lifelong friend) led to him becoming a Fellow of the Royal Society in 1766, and to the publication of his *History of Electricity* in 1767.

Priestley gave up being a clergyman in 1773 – he decided he could serve God better through science – and went to work for the Earl of Shelbourne, who was happy to fund Priestley's research in return for his services as tutor, librarian and 'literary companion', in which latter capacity he accompanied Shelbourne to France in 1774.

Priestley was now an established 'natural philosopher' (in today's terminology, a 'physicist'), and while in Paris he called on Lavoisier, the great French chemist. The previous year, Lavoisier had begun experimenting on tin and lead, and discovered that air itself was responsible for the increase in weight of the metals when they were heated. But what was in the air that caused this increase? The answer, we now know, is oxygen, and Priestley is often credited (in Britain at least) with its discovery. However, though he had in fact isolated oxygen, he had no conception that it was a new element. He told Lavoisier it was 'an air five or six times as good as common air', and called it 'dephlogisticated air' (phlogiston being a substance then thought to leave every physical body when it was burnt). Lavoisier realized Priestley was onto something and in 1779 came up with the name 'oxygen'. Strictly, however, neither Priestley nor Lavoisier (nor the other contemporary candidate, the Swedish scientist Scheele) can be said to have actually discovered oxygen as we know it today.

Nevertheless, Priestley appreciated the interdependence of animal and plant life, and the meeting with Lavoisier helped him establish how all living things are linked through respiration: 'the injury which is continually done to the atmosphere by [animals is] in part at least, repaired by the vegetable creation.' Our modern debate about ecology and climate change is ultimately founded upon the discussion between these two men.

What happened next
Lavoisier, like Priestley, was a friend of Franklin, and used his political influence and scientific knowledge to help the American Revolution (his work on gunpowder was very handy). Come the French Revolution, however, Marat (☞ SEE 41), who disliked Lavoisier, ensured he ended up on the guillotine in 1794. As the mathematician Lagrange commented, it took an instant to strike off a head that a 'hundred years may not produce'. Priestley stayed a believer in both phlogiston and revolution for the rest of his life: his defence of the French Revolution, in reply to Burke (☞ SEE 31), resulted in a Birmingham mob burning his house. He moved to Pennsylvania, where he died in 1804, confidently awaiting Christ's Second Coming.

— 33 —

1775: ROBESPIERRE MAKES A SPEECH TO LOUIS XVI (AND GETS VERY WET)

One of the most haunting scenes in the history of the 18th century features the schoolboy Robespierre standing in the rain, waiting for the coach carrying Louis XVI and Marie-Antoinette to arrive at the gates of his school, Louis-Le-Grand, where the boy would deliver an address on behalf of the staff and pupils.

Robespierre had arrived at the prestigious school from provincial Arras thanks to a scholarship, and the boy's seriousness of purpose made a great impression on his teachers, one of them calling him 'my Roman'. The 'Roman' was the obvious representative to make a speech to the king, but someone's timing was out. For two hours, the boy waited and waited, getting wetter and wetter. The coach finally arrived and stopped beside the shivering boy, who knelt and read out the speech of welcome to the king. What Louis said or even looked like at this moment is impossible to say, as although the coach door was open, the curtains were kept firmly closed. Louis received the speech in silence; and, when it was over, the coach drove off (this does put Louis in a poor light, but he was a shy monarch).

There was to be no further encounter until the king's trial, so Louis – warm and safe as he was behind his coach curtains – was to have no visual memory of the boy who was to grow into the man who was to send him and his loved ones to the scaffold in 1793. Robespierre argued at the trial of 'citizen Louis Capet' (as the dethroned Louis was known by the revolutionaries), that the purpose of the trial was not to pass sentence on an individual but to protect the state. The 'fatal truth' was that Capet should die to protect the lives of thousands of virtuous French citizens: Louis had to die in order that the Revolution should live.

Robespierre was against capital punishment in principle. but the 'incorruptible' one was prepared to make the noble sacrifice of accepting purely temporary exemptions to that principle for the sake of the state. Robespierre did not attend the execution of the ex-monarch he once loyally addressed in the rain, but stayed home. As the coach carrying the ex-king passed his residence, Robespierre shooed a young girl in his house away from the window, closed the shutters and told the child that something was happening 'which you should not see'.

What happened next

Thousands were to die during Robespierre's 'Terror', until the wave of killing consumed the man himself. Those who escaped by chance included the Marquis de Sade (☞ SEE 36) and Tom Paine. Then Napoleon took power, and after his final defeat Louis's Bourbon dynasty was restored, having, as the side-switching statesman Talleyrand observed, 'forgotten nothing and learned nothing'.

—34—

1776: DR JOHNSON HAS DINNER WITH JOHN WILKES, AND THEY COMPARE NOTES ABOUT SCOTS

Dr Johnson was a staunch Tory, conservative in his religion and politics, yet passionately opposed to slavery, one of his many reasons for disliking Americans. John Wilkes was one of the leading radicals of the age, a Whig, and a notorious libertine to boot. Johnson's biographer, the ever-inquisitive James Boswell, was friends with them both, and he said: 'Two men more different could perhaps not be selected out of all mankind.' They had even attacked one another with real venom in print, and Boswell decided to orchestrate a meeting by arranging that they should sit beside each other at a dinner party at a friend's house.

Boswell cleverly 'negotiated' Johnson for the encounter by telling him that their host might have radical friends present: 'I should not be surprised to find Jack Wilkes there.' Johnson said: 'And if Jack Wilkes SHOULD be there, what is that to ME, Sir? My dear friend, let us have no more of this. I am sorry to be angry with you; but really it is treating me strangely to talk to me as if I could not meet any company whatever, occasionally.' At the friend's house, Johnson was disconcerted to find himself surrounded by radicals and 'patriots' ('Patriotism is the last refuge of a scoundrel', he once noted), but when they were called into dinner, Boswell says Wilkes 'placed himself next to Dr Johnson, and behaved to him with so much attention and politeness, that he gained upon him insensibly. No man eat more heartily than Johnson, or loved better what was nice and delicate. Mr Wilkes was very assiduous in helping him to some fine veal. 'Pray give me leave, Sir:–It is better here–A little of the brown–Some fat, Sir–A little of the stuffing–Some gravy–Let me have the pleasure of giving you some butter–Allow me to recommend a squeeze of this orange;–or the lemon, perhaps, may have more zest.'–'Sir, Sir, I am obliged to you, Sir,' cried Johnson, bowing, and turning his head to him with a look for some time of "surly virtue", but, in a short while, of complacency.'

The two even discovered a mutual antipathy to Scots, England being then – as at some other times – run by unpopular Caledonians. Johnson said to Wilkes: 'You must know, Sir, I lately took my friend Boswell and shewed him genuine civilized life in an English provincial town. I turned him loose at Lichfield, my native city, that he might see for once real civility: for you know he lives among savages in Scotland, and among rakes in London.' Wilkes replied: 'Except when he is with grave, sober, decent people like you and me.' Johnson smiled in response.

What happened next
Wilkes and Johnson briefly met once more, years later, again under Boswell's eye, and again they got on. Boswell's experiment had worked, but only as far as it went. Wilkes does not seem to have shared Johnson's visceral disgust at slavery (Johnson once drank a toast to the next slave rebellion) and by an odd quirk of fate the assassin of Abraham Lincoln, John Wilkes Booth, a passionate defender of slavery, was named after him.

~35~

1777: PATRICK FERGUSON DECIDES NOT TO SHOOT GEORGE WASHINGTON WITH HIS NEWFANGLED RIFLE

Early in the American War of Independence, a young British captain (accompanied by three riflemen) was scouting the American lines by the Brandywine Creek in Pennsylvania. He was a Scots Greys officer called Patrick Ferguson, and he and his men were armed with the rifle he had invented, the world's first breech-loader.

Two horsemen appeared riding towards Ferguson's hidden group, one a decoratively clad hussar, the other a senior American officer. Ferguson's first thought was to shoot the two men, but feeling this was a 'disgusting' idea, he emerged from cover and called on the hussar, who was nearest, to dismount. The enemy riders instead rode for the safety of their lines. Ferguson and his men could each get off six accurately aimed rounds a minute and could almost certainly have killed both men, but instead Ferguson let the tempting figure of the senior officer go. He later said: 'I could have lodged a half dozen balls in or about him before he was out of my reach ... but it was not pleasant to fire at the back of an unoffending individual who was acquitting himself coolly of his duty, and so I let him alone.'

This happened four days before the Battle of the Brandywine. Ferguson was wounded during the battle (which the British won, then captured Philadelphia), and was told in hospital that the officer he had let live was George Washington. The story was doubted for a long time, because of the presence of the mysterious hussar, as there were no such soldiers with the American forces. In fact, the 'hussar', it turns out, was a Polish count called Pulaski (recruited in Paris by Benjamin Franklin), who was serving as Washington's aide-de-camp. Washington had been out inspecting his lines with Pulaski, so he was almost certainly the man whom Ferguson declined to kill.

Ferguson's background was that of the Scottish Enlightenment: his family lived on Edinburgh's High St, and knew everybody who mattered, from the philosopher David Hume to the painter Allan Ramsay. But his decision to spare Washington was based on an older chivalric soldier's ethic; at Waterloo, Wellington declined a similar opportunity to shell Napoleon (an attitude that soon died out).

What happened next
Ferguson's highly advanced rifle was rejected by the army as a 'barbarous' weapon, but what if he had indeed shot Washington with it? Many Americans believe that the failure of the Revolution would have been a disaster for humanity. Arguably, it is more likely that American slaves would have gained their freedom without a civil war, colonial expansion into Indian lands would have halted, and North America would today be one huge Canadian nation down to the Mexican border; possibly a bit boring, but hardly a disaster. As for the gallant Ferguson, he was killed at the Battle of King's Mountain in 1780, in which he was the only non-American combatant. His body was stripped and urinated on by the Patriot militia before being passed to his orderly for cleaning and burial. Ferguson was buried on King's Mountain beside his female servant and companion, 'Virginia Sal', a 'buxom redhead' who was killed while tending the wounded and is, alas, not mentioned on Ferguson's headstone, erected in 1930.

─ 36 ─

1777: THE MARQUIS DE SADE INSULTS COUNT MIRABEAU

In 1777 the young Count Mirabeau was an ex-soldier with a reputation for indiscipline and intrigue who had run off with another man's wife, and ended up imprisoned in Vincennes prison. In prison with him was another nobleman, one with a much worse reputation, the Marquis de Sade. Sade was known to have (accidentally) poisoned prostitutes with the supposed aphrodisiac

'Spanish fly', had engaged in just about every vice known to French society, and was seen as a serious menace to the public.

The two men hated each other. Sade, who seems to have fought with everyone in prison and tried to instigate a revolt, shouted down from his cell window at the new arrival, who was exercising in the yard, accusing him of unnatural sexual preferences (a bit rich, really, coming from Sade) and threatening to hack off Mirabeau's ears. Mirabeau responded by saying that the only fear he had was that Sade would be executed before he could get his hands on him. Vincennes was a tough prison, even for aristocrats who could buy favours in jail. Normally the two quarrelsome aristos would have paid off a warder and settled their dispute with a duel, but in Vincennes all they could do was avoid each other for the next three years, apart from the occasional glare (Mirabeau gleefully endorsed his 1780 release on the back of the record of Sade's incarceration).

In their separate cells they passed the time by writing fiction, which, depending on one's view, falls into the category of erotica or pornography. Over the next ten years or so, Sade produced *The 100 Days of Sodom*, a heroic attempt at cataloguing every perversion known to man, *Justine, Crimes of Passion*, and *Dialogue Between a Priest and a Dying Man*, a philosophical treatise in praise of atheism. Mirabeau's writing in and out of jail was a bit more moderate. His works include *Erotica Biblion* and *Letters to Sophie*, 'Sophie' being his pet name for the woman he had run off with (the real Sophie, ungallantly dismissed in the 1911 *Britannica* as 'rather common', committed suicide).

What happened next
Mirabeau became one of France's leading orators, and a leading (if also corrupt) moderate during the French Revolution. He was interred with great pomp in the Pantheon after his death in 1791, then dug up three years later and reinterred elsewhere when his duplicity became apparent. Sade was transferred to the Bastille in 1784, and from thence to Charenton Asylum just before the storming of the Bastille in July 1789. Given his freedom by the French Revolution, he was appointed a judge and a member of the National Convention but was imprisoned again – for being too moderate! – and, like

many others, missed the guillotine by a fluke. Napoleon called for his arrest in 1801, and he returned to Charenton, where he put on plays until his death in 1814.

—37—

1781: BENJAMIN FRANKLIN MEETS CATHERINE DASHKOVA

Catherine Dashkova was born a countess in Russia, had married a prince at 15, and at the age of 18 may have played a part in the coup which brought Catherine the Great to the throne in 1762. Benjamin Franklin was one of the world's leading statesmen: a diplomat, scientist, inventor, and author.

Yet they had more in common than it seems. Catherine had been a sickly child and became a voracious reader, and there is no doubt about her intelligence and breadth of knowledge. However, she did not quite get on with the empress – Catherine despised the talentless male court favourites, and also seems to have been peeved not to be appointed colonel of the Imperial Guard – so she went to Europe for a few years, where she became a friend of Enlightenment thinkers such as Diderot and Voltaire (and later sent her son to Edinburgh University). She had a degree in mathematics and also wrote plays. She was not of course in the same league as the dauntingly polymathic Franklin, but was closer to it than most, then or now.

Catherine, aged 37, and Franklin, then 75, met socially in Paris and took to each other straight away. While older men have often had their heads turned by younger women, Franklin's later invitation to Catherine to join the American Philosophical Society in 1789 was not given lightly (it would be 80 years before another woman was invited). This was the only time they met, though they were to exchange affectionate letters and notes over the years, and Catherine reciprocated Franklin's invitation by arranging for him to join the Russian Academy of Sciences in St Petersburg later that year (she founded the Academy, and was its first president): 'I was greatly surprised [she wrote], when reviewing the list of its members some days ago, I did not find your name in the number. I hastened therefore to acquire this honour for the academy... I shall always recollect with pride the advantage I had to be personally noticed by you.'

What happened next

Catherine returned to Russia in 1782, to a warm welcome from the empress. When the monarch died in 1796, however, the new emperor meanly imposed village exile on Dashkova, evidently in belated punishment for whatever she had done in 1762. After another coup, she was allowed back to Moscow, and died there in 1810. Her memoirs were published in London in 1840. Her brief encounter with Franklin had some surprising international consequences. She knew that Russia had to modernize, and promoted the works of Franklin and other Enlightenment thinkers throughout the country's institutions, which influenced many practical aspects of Russian life, including the development of the Imperial Navy. Russia subsequently became an important ally of the new US nation and would play an important part in the result of the Civil War, during which the Russian fleet acted – astonishing as it seems – as a de facto Pacific fleet for the Union, preserving its western flank from naval attack.

~38~

1786: WALTER SCOTT MEETS ROBERT BURNS, AND IS IMPRESSED BY HIS EYE

Burns was born and brought up on an Ayrshire farm, and at 16 was his father's principal labourer. While working, he 'listened to the birds, and frequently turned out of my path lest I should disturb their little songs or frighten them to another station'. The 1911 *Britannica* waxes rapturously on the young Burns, 'Auroral visions were gilding his horizon as he walked in glory, if not in joy' (Burns has always attracted this kind of commentary).

In 1786, at the age of 27 and his father two years dead, Burns was on the point of departing for Jamaica, to work as an overseer on a

Scottish slave plantation, when he achieved instant success with the publication of the great 'Kilmarnock' edition of his verse. Before publication, Burns had envisaged that news of any success would not reach him in Jamaica: 'twas a delicious idea that I would be called a clever fellow, even though it should never reach my ears a poor Negro-driver.'

In Edinburgh, Burns was patronized (in every sense) by the aristocracy, notably the Earl of Glencairn, who introduced the brilliant young poet to his circle of friends. One shy young boy present at one of these gatherings was the future novelist Walter Scott, then aged 15, who later recalled: 'I... had sense enough to be interested in his poetry, and would have given the world to know him. I saw him one day with several gentlemen of literary reputation... Of course we youngsters sat silent, looked, and listened... His person was robust, his manners rustic, not clownish... His countenance was more massive than it looks in any of the portraits. There was a strong expression of shrewdness in his lineaments; the eye alone indicated the poetic character and temperament. It was large and of a dark cast, and literally glowed when he spoke with feeling or interest. I never saw such another eye in a human head... He was much caressed in Edinburgh, but the efforts made for his relief were extremely trifling.'

What happened next
The success of his poems persuaded Burns to stay in Scotland, where he was to become, after his death ten years later, one of the country's iconic figures, and Scott's account of him has been quoted ever since. If the Kilmarnock edition had failed, however, there is little doubt Burns would have been off to Jamaica and Scott would have missed seeing that fine eye. It is habitual for admirers of Burns to slide over the implications of the 'negro-driver' comment, but the truth is that the horrors of the Scottish slave plantations were well-known in Scotland, and it is implausible that Burns was unaware of them. Indeed, William Creech, the publisher of the Edinburgh edition of his poems, was an active anti-slavery campaigner. Burns did write, in 1792, a much-quoted poem on the horrors of slavery,

'The Slave's Lament', not a great poem in itself but a fine piece of anti-slavery rhetoric.

~39~

1788: OLAUDAH EQUIANO PRESENTS A PETITION TO QUEEN CHARLOTTE

Olaudah Equiano was a freed slave who had suffered much hardship in his early life, eventually buying his freedom in 1766, aged 21. He became involved in the anti-slavery movement in England and was appointed Commissary of Provisions and Stores for the ill-starred Sierra Leone project, which the government set up in the hope of resettling freed Africans back in Africa (probably making him Britain's first high-level black civil servant). Equiano discovered wholesale corruption in the project, and despite the backing of the Navy Board, was sacked in 1787 (he was subsequently vindicated).

As Equiano tells us in his memoir, *The Interesting Narrative of the Life of Olaudah Equiano, or Gustavus Vassa, the African* (1789), in 1788 he presented a petition on Africa's plight to Queen Charlotte, which was 'received most graciously by her Majesty'. Equiano's memoir was in fact well-subscribed before publication, and two of the subscribers were Charlotte's sons, the Prince of Wales and the Duke of York. Equiano was popular, well-connected, much sought after as an acquaintance, and recognized as a man of culture and learning (qualities not always present among Georgian gentlemen).

The petition (reprinted in the memoir) is of great significance as previous anti-slavery petitions to the royal family had not been so graciously received. Thanks to campaigners such as Wilberforce, Clarkson and Granville Sharp, the climate was changing: Equiano was an African who had been sold into slavery, but he was also clearly an English gentleman whose words could not be ignored: 'I supplicate your Majesty's compassion for millions of my African countrymen, who groan under the lash of tyranny in the West Indies ... by your Majesty's benevolent influence, a period may now be put to their misery; and they may be raised from the condition of brutes, to which they are at present degraded, to the rights and situation of freemen'.

What happened next

Equiano's assertion that he was born in Africa, and taken across the Atlantic as a child has become a matter of some debate. It seems likely that he was born in South Carolina, but when contemporary pro-slavery interests tried to discredit Equiano, the tactic failed. If Equiano had conflated the experience of others with his own, then it was no big deal to the British people, who were inexorably turning against slavery. Equiano became a rich man, and married and had two children. The black population of London was actually proportionately larger than in modern times, and they didn't go away: like Equiano, they married white women and their descendants are often unaware of their African ancestry (in 1817, Jane Austen made no great issue of introducing a 'half-mulatto' heiress into her unfinished novel *Sanditon*). And in a final twist to the encounter between Equiano and Charlotte, Queen Charlotte herself is often said to be of African descent (as of course, going further back, are we all).

— *40* —

1792: JOSEPH BRANT THE MOHAWK CHIEF MEETS GEORGE WASHINGTON

When George Washington met the Mohawk chief Joseph Brant (aka Thayendanegea, 'he who places two bets'), it was no kind of 'noble savage' he was meeting. As has been said, one of the pair was a well-travelled and sophisticated gentleman with high social connections, who had his portrait painted by George Romney – the other was George Washington. And while they were both freemasons, Brant had been handed his apron by King George III himself.

Brant had visited London in 1776, and he was interviewed by James Boswell (always watching for the man of the hour) for the *London*

Magazine. Brant's society friends were horrified to hear he was staying at an inn called 'The Swan With Two Necks', and tried to get him to move, but he was happy to remain at the Swan, where he was treated with 'much kindness'. Brant was by no means an oddity in London: many American Indians and blacks visited and often settled in England, where they tended to find their white neighbours friendlier than the ones back home.

Brant returned to America and led the Mohawk warriors in the bloody war against the rebels. The fighting was brutal and atrocities were common during the war, some being committed by Brant's Mohawks, though he, like many leaders on both sides, sought to prevent unnecessary killing. The Mohawk attacks were subsequently used by Americans to justify post-revolutionary punitive expeditions against Indians, though there are many parallel instances of patriot militiamen slaughtering defenceless loyalists and their Indian allies (especially in the war's immediate aftermath).

After the rebel victory in 1783, Brant told the British secretary of state that when he joined the English at the beginning of the war, it was 'purely on account of my forefathers' engagements with the king. I always looked upon these engagements, or covenants between the king and the Indian nations, as a sacred thing: Therefore, I was not to be frightened by the threats of the rebels at that time; I assure you I had no other view in it, and this was my real case from the beginning'.

In 1792, Brant was invited to meet Washington in Philadelphia. Washington hoped that Brant would use his good influence to broker peace with the Indian nations now fighting the Americans along the Ohio river. Washington offered Brant lands and a pension, which Brant immediately rejected as an obvious bribe. He agreed to intercede but he was being given an impossible task, as he well knew. The Indian tribes were not natural allies, the British (in Canada) were being duplicitous, and everyone knew that Washington was just buying time; the expansion into Indian lands, one of the stated aims of the War of Independence, would continue, no matter what.

What happened next.

Brant took ill and his mission was delayed. He did his best to work out a compromise agreement between the Indians and the Americans, but negotiations ended when the Indian alliance demanded the withdrawal of Americans to behind the Ohio river. War followed, and the Indians were heavily defeated at the Battle of Fallen Timbers in 1794. Brant, a devout Anglican, and a hero of Canada, died in 1807.

☛ SEE ALSO *35) Patrick Ferguson decides not to shoot George Washington with his newfangled rifle; 66) Queen Victoria meets Black Elk.*

⟶ 41 ⟶

1793: CHARLOTTE CORDAY ASSASSINATES MARAT IN HIS BATH

Charlotte Corday was born into a minor French aristocratic family and educated in a convent. Like many other young idealists, she became a supporter of the French Revolution in its early stages, seeing it as a benevolent process for social change. She belonged to the moderate 'Girondin' faction of the Revolution, and would have agreed with Wordsworth's French friend Beaupuy, who features in Wordsworth's autobiographical poem *The Prelude*, pointing to a hungry girl, saying 'Tis against that/ Which we are fighting'.

However, the 'September Massacres' of 1792, in which hundreds of imprisoned men, women and children were butchered by Paris mobs, transformed the views of moderates such as Corday. To quote Wordsworth again: 'I thought of those September massacres... /And felt and touched them, a substantial dread'. The Revolution had, for many former supporters, become monstrous.

Corday resolved to kill Jean-Paul Marat, one of the most extreme of the revolutionary leaders. Like most advocates of terror, Marat liked compiling lists of his enemies, and Corday requested a meeting, offering to inform on disaffected Girondins. Corday purchased a knife and wrote a justification of her plan to kill Marat, addressed to the people of France. On the evening of 13 July, Marat, who suffered from a bad skin condition, received Corday while he sat in his bathtub, and began writing down the names of the supposed traitors as she recited them. Then Corday brought out her knife and stabbed him in the chest. He called out, 'À moi, ma chère amie!' ('Help me, my dear friend!') before dying. Jacques-Louis David's painting of this event, *The Death of Marat*, remains one of the iconic images of the revolution: the martyr-like Marat hangs over the side of the bath with the list in his hand; he has died while working for the people, murdered by an enemy of the people. Corday is excluded from the painting. In a much later painting by a lesser talent, Paul Baudry, Corday is portrayed as a dignified, virginal tyrannicide, standing over the slumped, scabrous corpse of Marat.

What happened next
Corday's trial was problematic for the regime: she was young, attractive, articulate, and many French people were cheering her (inwardly at least). The Tribunal tried to solve the problem by ordering her defence counsel to enter a plea of insanity, which reduced the proceedings to a farce. Corday defiantly declared she had killed not a man but a wild beast, and that she had killed him that others might live – a provocative jibe at the rhetoric of revolutionary martyrdom. Corday was guillotined and the executioner's assistant stunned the watching, and by now pretty hardened, crowd by slapping Corday's detached head. Thousands more Girondins, and other moderates and royalists, were to die in the following months, a period known appropriately as 'The Terror', which would last till the arrest and execution of Robespierre in July 1794.

☛ SEE ALSO *31) 1774: **Edmund Burke is enraptured by Marie-Antoinette.***

—42—

1797: NAPOLEON INVITES TOM PAINE TO DINNER AND ASKS HIM HOW TO INVADE ENGLAND

The status of the American War of Independence as a 'just war' is more debatable than it once seemed, but it is certainly clear that the English radical Tom Paine's significant contribution to its success has been largely written out of American history. George Washington ordered Paine's pamphlet, *The American Crisis*, to be read to the troops before the Battle of Trenton: 'These are the times that try men's souls. The summer soldier and the sunshine patriot will, in this crisis, shrink from the service of their country; but he that stands by it now, deserves the love and thanks of man and woman.' With brave words such as these, Paine inspired the American revolutionaries to continue when all seemed lost.

Paine, internationally recognized as a leading radical, would later travel to France, become a French citizen in 1792 and a member of the revolutionary National Convention, and narrowly escape the guillotine during 'The Terror'. By 1797 he had come to the conclusion that France should make war on England and 'free' its people. Napoleon, not yet emperor, but fresh from his stunningly successful Italian campaign, called on Paine to invite him to dinner (a dinner which it seems never took place). Napoleon introduced himself as a staunch republican and a defender of equality – indeed, he claimed that he slept with Paine's *The Rights of Man* under his pillow (we know from another source that Napoleon claimed he also slept with the faux-Celtic works of 'Ossian' under his pillow, but pillows were large in those days ...). He also said that he wanted a golden statue to be built of Paine in honour of his influence on the age, and invited him to suggest ways of invading England. Paine, one hopes not too much swayed by the offer of a golden statue, then wrote a couple of essays on how to organize the invasion, which envisaged the inclusion of a thousand gunboats.

He wrote to Thomas Jefferson later, 'the intention of the expedition was to give the people of England an opportunity of forming a government for themselves, and thereby bring peace'. As one of Paine's early biographers pointed out, Paine suggested Norfolk for one of the landing points: the Thetford-born Paine may have had 'a happy vision of standing once more in Thetford and proclaiming liberty throughout the land'.

What happened next
Napoleon did not, of course, choose to attack England, but invaded Egypt instead. In September 1798, Paine, now also exasperated by the American republic, published a plan in a French newspaper for its conquest. Paine returned to America in 1802, and was unsurprisingly booed in New York for his political opinions and free-thinking religious beliefs; even his friend Jefferson was cool. Paine died in 1809 and was buried in New Rochelle, New York State. In 1819 the English radical William Cobbett dug his bones up and took them back to England, prompting a vicious epigram from Byron:

> In digging up your bones, Tom Paine,
> Will. Cobbett has done well:
> You visit him on earth again,
> He'll visit you in hell.

Paine's bones subsequently disappeared, though the jawbone was said to be in Brighton in the 1930s. A gold-coloured statue of Paine (holding *The Rights of Man* upside down for some reason) was erected in Thetford in 1964.

REGENCY
and VICTORIAN
ENCOUNTERS
(19th CENTURY)

— 43 —

1805: SIR ARTHUR WELLESLEY SEES TWO SIDES OF NELSON

The Duke of Wellington and Admiral Nelson feature on most lists of famous Brits, and they did actually once meet. In 1834, in the presence of some friends who had been discussing the 'egotism and vanity' of Nelson, Wellington observed that 'Lord Nelson was, in different circumstances, two quite different men, as I myself can vouch, though I only saw him once in my life, and for, perhaps, an hour.' He recollected the meeting in September, 1805, in a waiting room at the Colonial Office, 14 Downing St., when both men were waiting to see Lord Castlereagh, the Secretary for War. Wellesley had just come back from nine years hard campaigning in India, and Nelson had returned from giving the French fleet a hard time in the West Indies. Wellington recalled his first sight of 'the gentleman, whom, from his likeness to his pictures and the loss of an arm, I immediately recognized as Lord Nelson. He could not know who I was, but he entered at once into conversation with me, if I can call it conversation, for it was almost all on his side and all about himself, and in, really, a style so vain and so silly as to surprise and almost disgust me. I suppose something that I happened to say made him guess that I was somebody, and he went out of the room for a moment, I have no doubt to ask the office keeper who I was, for when he came back he was altogether a different man, both in manner and matter. All that I had thought a charlatan style had vanished, and he talked of the state of this country and the probabilities of affairs on the Continent with a good sense, and a knowledge of subjects both at home and abroad, that surprised me equally and more agreeably than the first part of our interview had done; in fact, he talked like an officer and a statesman ... and certainly, for the last half or three-quarters of an hour, I don't know that I ever had a conversation that interested me more ... I saw enough to be satisfied that he was really a very superior man; but certainly a more sudden and complete metamorphosis I never saw.'

What happened next

Given that Wellington himself was described as a man for whom 'no dose of flattery was too strong for him to swallow', some contemporaries felt that his initial view of Nelson as a man with a high conceit of himself was a bit rich, but posterity has been kinder to Wellington – he is still regarded as an honourable foe, from India to France – than to Nelson, a man over whose reputation hangs the shadow of what Wordsworth called the 'great crime' of the handing over of radicals in Naples in 1799 for torture and execution, a shadow which has if anything grown darker over the years.

~ 44 ~

1810: TOM MOLINEAUX THE BLACK BOXER FIGHTS TOM CRIBB THE 'BLACK DIAMOND'

The circumstances under which the black American boxer Tom Molineaux came to England in 1810 remain obscure, and indeed he remains a little-known figure. Having somehow won his freedom in America, he arrived in England, where he was taken under the wing of another black American boxer, Bill Richmond, who owned a pub and boxing academy near Leicester Square. Richmond, who had been narrowly beaten by the great English boxer Tom Cribb, was quick to see Molineaux's potential, and arranged a prizefight with Cribb in December 1810. Curiously, Cribb was nicknamed the 'Black Diamond', an epithet often given subsequently to black sportsmen – Cribb got it because he used to be a coalman.

It is difficult now to appreciate just how very popular prizefights were in England at the time, and the fight for the best bare-knuckle boxer in England was effectively the world championship of the day. The English cheerfully adopted their favourite boxers as symbols of national patriotism in the struggle against Napoleon, including not just black boxers such as Molineaux but also the great Jewish boxer (and former champion) Daniel Mendoza, as this popular ballad shows:

Mendoza, Gully, MOLINEAUX,
Each nature's weapon wield,
Who each at Boney would stand true,
And never to him yield.

The Molineaux-Cribb bout lasted 33 brutal rounds. At the end of each round, the boxer had to come up 'to scratch', indicating readiness to continue, and after 28 rounds Cribb – sensationally – failed to come up, but was saved by completely bogus complaints from his seconds. Cribb was also helpless against the ropes on one occasion, when someone cut them. Molineaux should have won the fight, but was defeated after 33 rounds of hard battering.

A justifiably aggrieved Molineaux obtained a rematch in September 1811, but had his jaw fractured in the 9th round, and collapsed in the 11th, in front of a wildly partisan crowd desperate for the Englishman to win a clear victory.

What happened next
Molineaux's fall from world-class boxer to freak-show exhibit was a sad one. His formidable physique and skill wilted as he drank his way round a series of grim exhibition bouts, and he eventually lost the support of his long-suffering patron Richmond. In 1819, in his mid-30s, the man who may have been one of the best heavyweight boxers ever died in Galway in the bandroom of the East Middlesex regiment, cared for by two of the regiment's black soldiers. On a happier note, Richmond, who should also be better known, became a much-respected figure about London (he was a fine cricketer and a friend of Byron), and was a page, with Cribb, at the coronation of George IV in 1821. It was no sinecure; Cribb and Richmond had to watch out for George's wife, Caroline, a potential gatecrasher who was barred from the ceremony. Richmond died in 1829 after an evening spent with Cribb.

~45~

1812: BEETHOVEN MEETS GOETHE (AND SNUBS THE AUSTRIAN EMPRESS)

The German poet and philosopher Goethe loved many women, and although the one he finally married seemed to many contemporaries to be just a pretty face, most of the women he admired were clever as well as good-looking. It was through the child of one of those women that the giant of German letters met Beethoven, the giant of German music. The mutual friend was a young woman called Bettina Brentano, and it has been conjectured that she may in fact have been Goethe's daughter. She was certainly very comfortable in his presence, and once fell asleep in his lap. Goethe never knew quite what to make of her (and neither did Napoleon when he met her).

In 1812, when all three were all present at the Teplitz Spa, Bettina introduced the two German giants to each other. It was while at the spa that Beethoven wrote his famous letter to the 'Immortal Beloved', a passionate note to an unknown woman, which was found after his death in 1827. Bettina had earlier, in 1810, introduced Beethoven to her relation Antonie Brentano, who is considered by some to have been this 'Beloved'.

In one of these scenes that seem too good to be true (and although recorded by Bettina, some feel it actually *is* too good to be true), Beethoven and Goethe were strolling arm-in-arm when they encountered the Empress of Austria and a gaggle of dukes coming in their direction. Beethoven – who had been holding forth on the superiority of men of genius to men of birth – told Goethe to keep his arm locked with his: 'They must make room for us, not we for them.' But Goethe's day job, after all, was as a courtier, and he found this impossible to do.

Goethe freed his arm from Beethoven's grasp, took off his hat, and bowed to the empress. Beethoven crossed his arms and kept walking, the dukes parting before him like the Red Sea before Moses. After

Goethe had bowed his way out, Beethoven told him he had waited for him because he honoured, indeed revered, Goethe for his mind, and told him off for bowing to talentless aristocrats. The scene has become emblematic of the emerging new age of Romantic genius trampling on outdated mores, and a splendid contemporary picture called *The Incident in Teplitz* depicts the scene in that light; Goethe bows reverentially, while Beethoven strides away with his head held high.

What happened next
Goethe wrote home that Beethoven was 'turbulent'; Beethoven told his publisher that Goethe was too enamoured of courts. Apart from their genius, they evidently had little in common. Bettina became quite radical in her politics and often strolled arm-in-arm with her great friend Karl Marx in the 1840s. A utopian commune established by Germans in Texas in 1847 was named 'Bettina' in her honour.

─46─

1814: HARRIETTE WILSON CHATS UP LORD BYRON

Harriette Wilson was a Regency courtesan and her *Memoirs* (1825) has one of the best opening lines ever: 'I shall not say why and how I became, at the age of fifteen, the mistress of the Earl of Craven.' Her first glimpse of Lord Byron, described by his ex-lover Lady Caroline Lamb as 'mad, bad, and dangerous to know', was at a masquerade. Harriette wandered into a quiet room and found him there, staring pensively into the middle distance. 'Surely he sees beyond this gay scene into some other world, which is hidden from the rest of mankind,' she thought, and felt 'I was in the presence of a supernatural being. His attitude was graceful in the extreme. His whole countenance so bright, severe, and beautiful, that I should have been afraid to love him.'

Harriette watched the beautiful stranger for another ten minutes before delivering this grandiloquent chat-up line: 'I entreat you to gratify my curiosity. Who and what are you, who appear to me a being too bright and too severe to dwell among us?'

A startled Byron (who had previously turned down an invitation to meet Harriette) replied that he was merely a 'very stupid masquerade-companion' and tried to escape, but Harriette was not letting him off so easily, telling him 'you must be Lord Byron, whom I have never seen'. 'And you,' said Byron, 'are Harriette Wilson.' They then had a pleasant time discussing beauty: 'Your beauty is all intellectual' she told him – and criticizing Lady Caroline Lamb – 'Is there any sort of comparison to be made between you and that mad woman?' he told her, and they parted with mutual admiration. Byron said, 'Wherever I am, it will console me to know that I am remembered kindly by you', and Harriette replied, 'God bless you, dear Lord Byron'.

Walter Scott described Harriette as a 'smart, saucy girl', which is how most people think of her. In fact she was a very fine writer with an eye for the ridiculous. The encounter with Byron is a parody of romantic fiction, a clever send-up of the moody 'Byronic' hero, a persona assiduously cultivated by Byron himself.

What happened next

A small packet of Harriette's letters to Byron was found in the 20th century, one with this charming request: 'I hate to ask you for money... However, I only require a little present aid, and that I am sure you will not refuse me, as you once refused to make my acquaintance because you held me too cheap.' No letters from him to her survive. Byron left England for good in 1816, and died at Missolonghi in 1824, preparing to fight for Greek independence. Harriette died in rich obscurity around 1845. Her memoirs may have earned her in excess of £10,000. Some men paid to be kept out. The Duke of Wellington's response to Harriette's publisher ('Publish and be damned!'), is, however, apocryphal.

—47—

1815: JANE AUSTEN VISITS THE PRINCE REGENT'S LIBRARIAN (WHO IS FULL OF SUGGESTIONS)

In late 1815, Jane Austen was nursing her brother Henry through a fever in his London house. Henry was also being attended by a royal physician who knew that his patient's sister was the anonymous author of *Pride and Prejudice* and *Mansfield Park*. The physician delightedly informed Miss Austen that the Prince Regent was a lover of her books and that he had taken the liberty of telling him that their author was in London – and the prince had asked his librarian, Mr Clarke, to 'wait upon' the author and 'pay her every possible attention.' Mr Clarke accordingly invited Miss Austen to visit the prince's library at Carlton House.

Miss Austen had very decided views on the Prince Regent: she did not like him, and she wondered at his wife Caroline 'calling herself "attached & affectionate" to a Man whom she must detest'. The library was a different matter, however. During the tour Clarke mentioned that if Miss Austen published another novel, she 'was at liberty' to dedicate it to the prince. At that moment, *Emma* was about to be published and, after she got home, Jane wrote asking Clarke if it was now 'incumbent' on her to inscribe the work to the prince: 'I should be equally concerned to appear either presumptuous or ungrateful.' Clarke wrote back that it was certainly not 'incumbent' but he was happy to confirm permission: 'And I also, dear Madam, wished to be allowed to ask you to delineate in some future work the habits of life, and character, and enthusiasm of a clergyman, who should pass his time between the metropolis and the country, who should be something like Beattie's Minstrel – "Silent when glad ... demurely sad".' Clarke seems not to have noticed that the clergymen in Jane Austen's novels tend to be rather dodgy characters. She replied: 'I am quite honoured by your thinking me capable of drawing such a clergyman as you gave the sketch of in your note of Nov. 16th. But I assure you I am not.'

An unperturbed Clarke replied with yet another suggestion: 'An historical romance illustrative of the august House of Cobourg would just now be very interesting.' Jane responded: 'I could not... write a serious romance under any other motive than to save my life... I am sure I should be hung before I had finished the first chapter. No, I must keep to my own style and go on in my own way; and though I may never succeed again in that, I am convinced that I should totally fail in any other.'

What happened next

As the novelist Reginald Hill has pointed out, *Emma* is one of the great English detective stories, and this extends even to the dedication. The author did indeed dedicate *Emma* to the Prince Regent, but her repeated use of the words 'His Royal Highness' may have been intended, as some claim, to remind readers of his estranged wife Caroline's use of the same words to address her husband. The Regent was eventually crowned George IV in 1821, when he hired England's best boxers to keep the unfortunate Caroline away from the event.

☛ SEE ALSO *44) 1810: Tom Molineaux the black boxer fights Tom Cribb the 'Black Diamond'*.

— 48 —

1817: BENJAMIN HAYDON HOSTS THE 'IMMORTAL DINNER'

Having moved into a new London studio in 1817, the painter Benjamin Haydon decided to bring a group of his friends together for a party, with his work-in-progress *Christ's entry into Jerusalem* functioning as a centrepiece. Present at the dinner were Wordsworth, Keats (their faces are on two of the figures in the painting, which now lives in an Ohio seminary), and Charles Lamb. Also present that evening was the surgeon Joseph Ritchie, and the deputy controller of stamps, a dull chap called John Kingston, who, says Haydon, 'the moment he was introduced he let Wordsworth know who he officially was,' thus rather rudely informing Wordsworth that he was meeting his boss (for the first and only time), Wordsworth being the official distributor of stamps for Westmorland.

'The Immortal Dinner' is Haydon's own description of the evening, though posterity is not quite so certain on just how significant, never mind 'immortal', the evening was. But this was the first time Wordsworth and Keats met, and it certainly deserves special note as one of the few recorded social occasions at which Wordsworth looked as if he were enjoying himself. Haydon records that Lamb and Keats agreed that Newton 'had destroyed all the poetry of the rainbow by reducing it to the prismatic colours'. They drank a poetical toast to 'Newton's health and confusion to mathematics'. Wordsworth was spotted 'giving in to all our frolics without affectation and laughing as heartily as the best of us'. With such a collection of geniuses letting their hair down, we can share Haydon's delight at 'seeing Wordsworth, sitting, and Keats and Lamb, and my picture of Christ's Entry towering up behind them ... and hearing the voice of Wordsworth repeating Milton with an intonation like the funeral bell of St Paul's and the music of Handel mingled, and then Lamb's wit ... sparkling in between, and Keats's rich fancy of satyrs and fauns and white clouds, [which] wound up the stream of conversation.'

Keats in fact was reciting part of his long mythological poem *Endymion* for the first time in company (Wordsworth had read it a few days earlier and praised it faintly). Lamb – whose sister Mary was in his care, having killed their mother years before in one of her periodic fits of madness – got a bit squiffy and attempted to examine the skull of John Kingston, who persisted in asking daft questions about genius. Lest there be any doubt as to the general propriety of the evening, however, Haydon makes clear: 'All our fun was within bounds. Not a word passed that an apostle might not have listened to. It was a night worthy of the Elizabethan age ...'

What happened next
Joseph Ritchie, who was an anti-slavery campaigner, died in Murzuq in November 1819, less than two years after the party. At Keats's request, Ritchie took with him a copy of *Endymion* in order to leave

it, for some mysterious poetical reason, in the Sahara. Haydon, the proud host, whose career was dogged by debt, committed suicide in the hot summer of 1846 (he shot himself, then cut his throat).

─49─

1822: SAN MARTIN AND SIMON BOLIVAR AGREE THERE IS ONLY ROOM FOR ONE LIBERATOR IN SOUTH AMERICA

Revered by Argentinians as the liberator of their country from Spanish rule, José de San Martin learned his military trade as an officer in the brutal war to liberate Spain from Napoleon's rule (1808-11). Deciding his talents could be better used fighting Spanish oppression at home after Argentina had declared its independence, he returned to Buenos Aires in 1812, where he became commander of the army. Realizing that Argentina would not be secure unless Spanish rule ended all over South America, he took an army across the Andes to liberate Chile (with local patriot Bernardo O'Higgins), founded the Chilean navy (with the Scot Thomas Cochrane) and became the 'Protector' (first president) of Peru not long before meeting Bolivar.

The Venezuelan Simon Bolivar had also been a busy man to the north in his part of the fight to remove Spanish rule, becoming temporary dictator of Venezuela in 1813. Unlike San Martin, Bolivar seems to have taken more naturally to the role of dictator. They arranged to meet, with San Martin as the liberator of the south, Bolivar the liberator of the north. The encounter – a secret one behind closed doors – was held in Ecuador at a time when they had Spain's mighty armies for the taking, and the purpose of the meeting was to plan the final strategy for the inevitable victory. The course of the meeting is still debated, but from what we know of what was said, it is difficult to view the great revolutionary Bolivar in anything but a bad light. San Martin offered at first to share the leadership; when Bolivar refused, on the grounds that his forces were the stronger, San Martin offered to step down. This noble offer, alas, also seems to have offended Bolivar, who probably at this point just wanted San Martin to have never existed. The Argentinian, realizing that Bolivar's intransigence was implacable, decided to turn over command to Bolivar, left South America for good and returned to Europe, dying in France in 1850.

What happened next
Bolivar went on to defeat the Spanish. Upper Peru was renamed Bolivia in his honour, but his ideal of a federation of all Spanish-speaking Americans never came to fruition and was probably never achievable, as he recognized on his deathbed in 1830, saying that the sole benefit of his work had been achieving independence from Spain, but at the cost of all other forms of civilized life. Life had become a torment, laws just bits of paper, and the future of South America would be one of governance by petty tyrants. Bolivar's unhappy prophecy was pretty much fulfilled. There were a series of wars in the 1860s and 1870s in which Chile and Peru fought with Spain, and later with Bolivia, over bird shit (the so-called 'Guano wars'). Also in the 1860s, Paraguay fought one of the most disastrous wars in history, fighting Argentina, Brazil and Uruguay at the same time (50-70% of Paraguay's population is estimated to have died).

~50~

1827: SCHUBERT VISITS BEETHOVEN ON HIS DEATHBED

By March 1827 Beethoven had been deaf for ten years, and was now dying in Vienna. He was 56 and widely regarded as the greatest living composer, as well as a symbol of both German culture and the Romantic movement (☞ SEE 45). The young Austrian composer Franz Schubert was also living in the city, but was painfully shy of making contact with the great man. Indeed, Schubert said he had once seen him in a busy coffee house but was too much in awe to go over to him (which rather puts in doubt claims, especially those spread by Schubert's brother, that Beethoven and Schubert met before 1827).

Beethoven had caught pneumonia, but he was dying anyway of liver failure (and possibly also lead poisoning). He had gone out to the country to visit his brother, who has been blamed for sending the ailing composer back to Vienna in an open wagon (Beethoven was actually very ill when he had arrived at the estate, where his erratic behaviour caused great amusement to the yokels).

When Schubert finally visited Beethoven on 19 March, he had only a few days to live. According to their mutual friend Anselm Huttenbrenner, Beethoven was asked which of the two he would like to see first: 'let Schubert come in first,' he replied. Beethoven was interested in the talented young composer's music, and probably would once have had much to say, but sadly by this point he was unable to speak lucidly (a cigarette card company later issued a series on Schubert's life, one of which shows a sobbing Schubert exiting the deathbed scene).

Shortly after Schubert left, Beethoven's voice returned and he spoke warmly of the Philharmonic Society of London, whose patronage had been of such importance to him. Earlier in 1827 he had written to the society explaining his financial problems and they sent him £100. George Bernard Shaw later referred to this gift as 'the only creditable incident in English history'. The Philharmonic had commissioned the 9th Symphony and wanted a 10th from him – practically his last words were 'God bless them'.

What happened next
'Who can do anything after Beethoven?' asked Schubert. Schubert's music does seem to change after this point, and biographers and musicologists agree that Beethoven's death is pivotal in Schubert's life and work, though he himself had less than a year to live. He was one of the torchbearers at Beethoven's funeral, which became a huge public event; over 20,000 people turned up to see him interred. Schubert died of syphilis (or, according to some reports, typhoid) at the age of 31 in 1828. At his own request, he was buried beside Beethoven.

~ 51 ~

1840: SIR MOSES MONTEFIORE MEETS SULTAN ABDÜLMECID TO DISCUSS THE 'DAMASCUS AFFAIR'

In February 1840, a Franciscan monk and his servant went missing in Damascus and were never seen again. Their disappearance resulted in rioting by Christians and Muslims who alleged that the missing men had been killed by Jews in order to use their blood for a ritual during Passover. Such allegations, known as the 'blood libel', have been used by fanatics to smear not only Jews, but other groups ranging from Cathars and neopagans to a wide range of Christian and Muslim sects that have annoyed the orthodox.

The disappearance of the two men coincided with the recent arrival in Damascus of a new French consul, one Ratti-Menton, who used his considerable influence to persuade the Turkish governor to arrest and interrogate local Jews. The consul did have a legal right to intervene – France having special rights as the protector of Roman Catholics in the region – but he was also a vicious anti-semite and the responsibility for much of what was to happen lies at the door of this horrible man. 'Suspects' were questioned, and several Jews died under torture; another converted to Islam to escape a similar fate. Anti-Jewish riots occurred all over the Middle East, in which Jews were attacked, and synagogues were desecrated.

The 'Damascus Affair', as it began to be called, quickly attracted worldwide attention and condemnation. After a public meeting in London offering support to the beleaguered Jewish communities, the prominent, well-connected and well-liked English Jew Sir Moses Montefiore, who was sheriff of the city of London and had been knighted by Queen Victoria, was appointed to lead a delegation to plead with Mehmet Ali, joint ruler (with the Ottoman Sultan) of Syria, for an end to the persecution. The delegation obtained the (reluctantly granted) release of the prisoners, but it was not until Montefiore went on to meet with the other ruler of Syria, the precocious 17-year-old Ottoman ruler Sultan Abdülmecid, in

Constantinople, that the persecutions ceased. Abdülmecid also, at Montefiore's request, issued a significant edict attacking the blood libel itself: 'For the love we bear to our subjects, we cannot permit the Jewish nation, whose innocence for the crime alleged against them is evident, to be worried and tormented as a consequence of accusations which have not the least foundation in truth.'

What happened next
'Normal' sectarian strife in Syria carried on as usual: in 1860, eight Franciscan monks in Damascus, the entire church community, were murdered by Druze zealots (and beatified in 1921), but the Sultan's edict against the blood libel held. Both of those remarkable men, Montefiore and Abdülmecid, have been largely forgotten, as has the Damascus Affair itself. Yet their encounter showed what could be achieved by rational and principled men prepared to stand up to bigotry. The affair led, alas, to a dramatic increase in anti-semitism everywhere, most notably in France and Russia. The blood libel is still propagated by some malignant clerics in the Middle East, most notably in Saudi Arabia, where the fable appeared as a factual description of Jewish ritual in a newspaper in 2002.

~52~

1842: EDGAR ALLAN POE ASKS CHARLES DICKENS TO HELP HIM GET PUBLISHED

Dickens toured America in 1842, and Poe came to see him twice in his Philadelphia hotel room. They talked a lot about copyright, a topic of much concern to authors but apt to drive most ordinary people out of the room. Accounts often resort to describing what they wore (Poe dressed in a respectable suit, Dickens went in for raffish diamond clasps and a flashy dressing gown).

Their relations started warmly enough. When Poe first requested a meeting, sending Dickens a collection of his stories as a gift, Dickens responded warmly: 'My Dear Sir, I shall be very glad to see you whenever you will do me the favour to call.' As well as discussing copyright, they talked of the possibility of Dickens finding a British publisher for Poe's short stories (this is the delicate part where one would like a verbatim account). Dickens, whatever his actual feelings on the subject, promised to try.

Poe's biographer Una Pope-Hennessy observes of the Poe and Dickens meetings that they were 'sterile and closed coldly. Neither seems to have liked the other much'. Neither were in good form when they met, but Poe was not (at any time) the most convivial of men, and while Dickens was normally good company, promising to try to find someone a publisher is a task not likely to end in joy. Dickens was certainly peeved at the level of exploitation he was encountering – the Philadelphia hotel, for example, conned him into presiding over a reception for hundreds of guests – and Poe's request may have seemed to be pitched on that level. In truth, however, he was profoundly depressed by America. He had come prepared to love the country but was deeply shocked by the reality of American slavery. He wrote: 'This is not the Republic I came to see. This is not the Republic of my imagination. I infinitely prefer a liberal Monarchy – even with its sickening accompaniments of Court Circulars... to such a Government as this.' His experiences were to be used to great satirical effect in *Martin Chuzzlewit* (1843). Dickens did meet Americans he really liked, however: Longfellow became a lifelong friend.

What happened next

Not long after returning to England, Dickens wrote to Poe that he had delivered his stories to various publishers but they all 'declined the venture'. Poe did derive one vital inspiration from Dickens. At the urging of his children, Dickens had put the family pet raven, Grip, into *Barnaby Rudge* (1841); Poe reviewed the book in May 1841 and criticized Dickens for not using the bird to good symbolic effect, which of course he himself was to do in his poem 'The Raven' (1845). Dickens had Grip stuffed when the bird died in 1841; Grip became known as 'Grip 1' as he had two successors. He was bought after Dickens' death by a Poe enthusiast who knew of the significance of the bird for Poe's work and donated him to the Free Library of Philadelphia, where he now lives on the third floor, a permanent memorial to both Poe and Dickens.

～53～

1854: JOHN LANG MEETS LAKSHMIBAI THROUGH A CURTAIN

Lakshmibai, Rani of Jhansi in north India, was a figure of some fascination to her Victorian contemporaries. A widow, she was ruler of the small north Indian kingdom of Jhansi, and was described as the 'Indian Boadicea'. She was attractive, intelligent, articulate, a stateswoman, and would become a symbol of resistance to the British during the Indian Mutiny of 1857, and has since become a national heroine for India.

The Sydney-born lawyer John Lang was a much less romantic figure, but is intriguing in his own right. Regarded as the first Australian-born novelist, he went to India in 1842, where he founded a newspaper, in which he published his novel *Mazarine* (1845).

Lakshmibai's husband, heir to a proud line of Maratha rulers, had died in 1853, and their only child was also dead. They had adopted a child whom the Rajah formally acknowledged as his heir before he died, but the British governor-general annexed the state anyway, under the so-called 'Doctrine of Lapse', which allowed the East India Company to take over a kingdom where the ruler died without a direct heir. Lakshmibai decided to fight the British at their own game and hired John Lang in 1854 to fight her case in the courts. Lang's enthralling account of their meeting was first published in Dickens' *Household Words*, and then in his *Wanderings in India* (1859).

Lang was taken to Jhansi in an enormous carriage escorted by spear-bearing cavalry, and then led on a white elephant to the palace. There he sat in a room with a curtain at the end, and spoke briefly to the 'pretty child' who was to inherit Jhansi, and who – perhaps accidentally – opened the curtain to reveal his mother the Rani expressing her grievances to Lang. He saw her only for a moment, but she clearly made an impression: he describes her as 'rather stout, but not too stout. Her face must have been very handsome when she was younger [she was then all of 25], and even now had many charms... The expression also was very good, and very intelligent'.

The next ten minutes passed with agreeable compliments from Lang to Lakshmibai. If the governor-general could only see her, Lang said, he felt 'quite sure that he would at once give Jhansi back again to be ruled by its beautiful Queen'. The 'beautiful Queen' stuck to the matter at hand, and declined Lang's suggestion that she take a British pension, saying in words that would resonate in Indian history: 'I will not give up my Jhansi.'

What happened next

Lang argued her case in London, but to no avail, and when rebellion broke out in 1857, Jhansi became a centre of the revolt. Lakshmibai encouraged women as well as men to take up arms against the imperialists, and fell in battle against the British at Gwalior in 1858. She has since become an Indian nationalist (and feminist) icon. A women's unit of the Indian National Army (the force raised by Japan from captured Indian troops and volunteers which fought – fiercely and effectively – against the British in Burma) was named after her.

~54~

1855: JAMES BARRY IS NASTY TO FLORENCE NIGHTINGALE

The 19th-century doctor James Barry, as the *Dictionary of National Biography* recognizes, 'was probably born Margaret', though she passed as a man throughout her adult life. She trained in medicine and became an experienced army surgeon and medical officer, eventually becoming a deputy inspector of hospitals. Like Mary Seacole (☞ SEE 56) she was discouraged from travelling to the Crimea when war broke out (on the grounds of being too senior, in Barry's case).

But Barry had influential friends, and when she put her case to the British commander Lord Raglan, he agreed she should be allowed to help. Barry was based on Corfu, and Raglan arranged for over 400 casualties to be sent to her for treatment. The recovery rates Barry achieved were high.

In 1855, Barry spent a few months leave (at her own expense) in Sevastopol, where she met Florence Nightingale. Barry was described at this time as an 'intolerable bore' who expected colleagues 'to listen to every quarrel he has had since coming into the service' (and there were many). Nightingale later recollected their encounter with a fair degree of spirit (Barry was annoyed with her about some trivial matter): 'I never had such a blackguard rating in all my life – I who have had more than any woman – than from this Barry sitting on his horse, while I was crossing the Hospital Square with only my cap on in the sun. He kept me standing in the midst of quite a crowd of soldiers, Commissariat, servants, camp followers, etc., etc., every one of whom behaved like a gentleman during the scolding I received while he behaved like a brute ... After he was dead, I was told that (he) was a woman ... I should say that (she) was the most hardened creature I ever met.'

What happened next
Barry is now generally regarded as transgendered: she was probably born a woman, and became a man by choice – a choice which benefited both medical science and her future patients, for Barry was a very fine doctor, though an argumentative and uncommonly uncivil one; indeed she had fought a duel in 1818 (though she and her opponent were unharmed). She died in 1865, aged about 66. The *Manchester Guardian* obituary said of Barry: 'He died about a month ago, and upon his death was discovered to be a woman. The motives that occasioned, and the time when commenced this singular deception are both shrouded in mystery. But thus it stands as an indisputable fact, that a woman was for 40 years an officer in the British service, and fought one duel and sought many more, had pursued a legitimate medical education, and received a regular diploma, and had acquired almost a celebrity for skill as a surgical operator. It was a supreme deception.' Indeed it was.

— 55 —

1855: ROBERT BROWNING IS UNENTRANCED BY DANIEL DUNGLAS HOME

The Spiritualist movement began in mid-19th century America with the emergence of 'mediums' who claimed to be in touch with a spirit world inhabited by nonmaterial beings. By 1853, when the song 'Spirit Rappings' was published ('Softly, softly, hear the rustle of the spirits' airy wings'), mediums were spreading all over America. One of them was Daniel Dunglas Home, a 22-year-old Scottish immigrant who believed his father was an illegitimate grandson of the Earl of Home. Home's aunt had thrown him out of the family home in Connecticut because she couldn't bear the frequent rapping which now accompanied his presence.

Mediumship was a viable career in those days, but Home, very much the gentleman, did not charge for seances; instead he consented to accept 'gifts'. Home returned in 1855 to a Britain in which spiritualism was meeting with increasing acceptance. He found sympathetic hosts to live with and regular seances to manage. Witnesses would even claim they saw Home float in and out of windows.

This brings us to what Andrew Lang, in *Historical Mysteries* (1904), called the 'great Home-Browning problem'. Elizabeth Barrett Browning admired Home and took her husband Robert Browning to one of his seances at the house of a Mr Rymer. Robert did not take to Home, and was not amused to receive what he called 'a kind of soft and fleshy pat' on his knee under the table (rumours about Home's sexuality abounded). A wreath of clematis floated up from the table and landed on the head of Elizabeth, which possibly amused Robert even less.

A few days later, Home called on the Brownings, but as Lang says: 'Mr Browning declined to notice Home; there was a scene, and Mrs

Browning (who was later a three-quarters believer in "spirits") was distressed.'

What happened next
Psychic research, according to Gladstone, was 'the most important work being done in the world today'. Others disagreed. After Elizabeth died, Robert lampooned Home in his 1865 poem 'Mr Sludge, the Medium'. 'When your departed mother spoke those words/ Of peace through me, and moved you, sir, so much,/ You gave me–(very kind it was of you) /These shirt-studs–(better take them back again ...)' Home retaliated by alleging that Browning was jealous because the spirits had judged Elizabeth the better poet by awarding her the clematis wreath. Home was later befriended by a widow who gave him a huge sum of money, but then demanded it back when the spirits told her to. The case went to court, where Home complained, 'I was a mere toy to her, I felt my degradation more and more with every day that passed'. The widow said: 'I once just put my lips to his forehead ... But only once. You see, I am not so fond of kissing.' The judge, describing spiritualism as 'mischievous nonsense', found against Home. Home married twice, converted twice (to Roman Catholicism and Greek Orthodoxy), was expelled from the city of Rome for necromancy, and died in France in 1886.

～56～

1855: MARY SEACOLE GETS A BED FOR THE NIGHT FROM FLORENCE NIGHTINGALE

When Mary Seacole was 'rediscovered' in the late 20th century, she was proclaimed as a heroine who had been 'written out' of British history because she was black and working-class, and therefore inferior to the white middle-class Florence Nightingale. The truth is more complex. Born Mary Grant in 1805 of Scottish-Creole parentage in Jamaica, where her mother ran a boarding-house for British officers, she married a merchant called Seacole in 1836.

Mary had expertise in treating fevers, and when war broke out with Russia in 1853, she travelled to England and offered her services to the War Office. Her offer was rejected (because of her colour, she believed) so she travelled to the Crimea herself to set up a base near the front line. On her way she visited Florence Nightingale at Scutari. Contrary to some sources, Mary did not ask for a job, as she makes clear in her autobiography, *The Wonderful Adventures of Mrs Seacole in Many Lands* (1857).

Mary describes Florence ('that Englishwoman whose name shall never die') as follows: 'A slight figure, in the nurses' dress; with a pale, gentle, and withal firm face, resting lightly in the palm of one white hand, while the other supports the elbow … Standing thus in repose, and yet keenly observant – the greatest sign of impatience at any time [was] a slight, perhaps unwitting motion of the firmly planted right foot.' Florence said 'in her gentle but eminently practical and business-like way, "What do you want, Mrs. Seacole – anything that we can do for you? If it lies in my power, I shall be very happy".' All Mary wanted was a bed, and one was found for her in the washerwoman's quarters. She left for the front in the morning.

Critics of Florence's supposedly superior attitude to Mary perhaps forget that Florence wanted to establish nursing as a profession, whereas Mary was running a business as well as nursing, and was therefore, in Florence's eyes, muddying the waters. Mary's business cards described her Crimean base – the British Hotel – as a 'mess-table and comfortable quarters for sick and convalescent officers'. Unlike Florence, Mary charged for her services, admitted tourists and served alcohol (though she used the profits to finance treatment of Russian as well as British soldiers). Florence was mostly polite about Mary, but privately she suggested that the British Hotel was a 'Bad House' (a euphemism for 'brothel') and she kept her nurses away.

What happened next
In his preface to Mary's book, *The Times* correspondent W H Russell says: 'I have witnessed her devotion and her courage … I trust that England will not forget one who nursed her sick, who sought out her wounded to aid and succour them, and who performed the last offices for some of her illustrious dead.' England did not

immediately forget. When Mary went bankrupt in 1856 a 'Seacole Fund', approved by Queen Victoria, was established to help her. Victoria's nephew Count Gleichen, whom she had treated in the Crimea, became a friend, and made a marble bust of her. Mary died of apoplexy in 1881, and thereafter Britain gradually forgot her.

─57─

1856: LOLA MONTEZ TRIES TO HORSEWHIP HENRY SEEKAMP

The legendary 'exotic' dancer Lola Montez was born in Sligo as Eliza Rosanna Gilbert, and was very pretty, as is evident from an 1848 portrait by the German artist Joseph Stieler. Some of the other 'Lola' portraits displayed in reference works are, however, not of Eliza at all. In the past it seems any old portrait of a sultry Spanish-looking woman wearing a jaunty hat would do to illustrate an article on Lola Montez. In fact, she had no Spanish ancestry, her father being a British soldier and her mother an illegitimate member of the well-known Irish Oliver family. She was indeed the mistress of a king – mad King Ludwig of I Bavaria – but did not, as is frequently alleged, die a terrible death.

Following a teenage elopement with one of her mother's friends, Eliza became 'Lola Montez, the Spanish dancer' in her early 20s, in which incarnation she debuted on the London stage in 1843. The performance ended in disorder after an aristocratic cad denounced her from his box as an Irish impostor. A few weeks later Lola turned up in continental Europe, where her 'tarantula dance' made her famous. She became King Ludwig's mistress in 1846, and he promoted her to countess in 1847. As often happened in Lola's life, her timing was bad: 1848 was the year of revolutions in Europe, and Ludwig was forced to abdicate.

Lola moved to the USA in 1851, where her dancing scandalized the righteous and delighted the rest, particularly in the goldfields of California. She moved to Australia in 1855, where her performances, in which she raised her skirt in front of the audience, proved too daring for family audiences, and indeed even for some of the 'digger' goldminers (Lola seemed to be drawn to the nearest goldmines, whatever continent she was on), who loved the eroticism, but were not prepared for Lola's willingness to trade insults with them.

Henry Seekamp, a major figure in both the history of Australian journalism and of its labour movement, was editor of the *Ballarat Times* and a noted supporter of the diggers in their struggle for their right to vote and buy the land they worked on. Seekamp is unfortunately best remembered outside of Australia for giving Lola a bad review, following which she chased him down the street with a horsewhip, thankfully without catching him. The still occasionally performed 'Lola Montes [*sic*] Polka', apparently commemorates this brief encounter.

What happened next

Lola's career was described in the *New York Times* as 'wonderfully chequered', and there are stories of a sad end in a squalid slum. In fact, she died of pneumonia in 1861, and was well cared for, but this was not good enough for the pious, who wanted to see a sinner brought low. It is not inappropriate to see her as a precursor of the modern, independent woman (with or without horsewhip). The most famous expression associated with her, 'Whatever Lola Wants, Lola Gets', may have arisen during her time as Ludwig's mistress, but it seems a fair summary of her lifestyle – and chimes with one view of the modern woman as assiduously courted by the advertising world.

~58~

1860: RICHARD BURTON JOKES ABOUT WIVES WITH BRIGHAM YOUNG

We now see Richard Burton as the very model of the intrepid Victorian explorer. By 1860 (aged 39) he had served as a soldier in India, visited Mecca (disguised as a Pathan), searched (with Speke) for the source of the Nile, and 'discovered' Lake Tanganyika. Burton, like many of his contemporaries, was fascinated by the Mormons, and travelled to Salt Lake City to find out more. As an early biographer says, 'it was natural that, after seeing the Mecca of the Mohammedans, Burton should turn to the Mecca of the Mormons, for he was always attracted by the centres of the various faiths'.

The trip is described in *The City of the Saints and across the Rocky Mountains to California* (1862), a book in which Burton is at pains to emphasize that Mormons must not be judged by our standards. Burton went to the Tabernacle, at that point a simple brick building, and after the service he was introduced to Brigham Young, the president of the Latter Day Saints, 'a farmer-like man of 45' who clearly knew his man. When Burton (who 'collected' religions) asked if he could become a Mormon, Young replied: 'I think you've done that sort of thing once before, Captain.'

They went for a stroll and exchanged pleasantries. Burton explained he was looking for a wife, but the Mormons had snapped them all up. Young showed Burton the house where his wives lived, and Burton made a slightly risqué remark about there being lots of water in Salt Lake City, but not 'a drop to drink'. Young, 'who loved a joke as dearly as he loved his 17 wives burst out into hearty laughter' (the true number of Young's wives remains uncertain – perhaps 27). Burton's quip was perhaps a bit daring, as he would have known of Young's brisk views on adultery: 'Suppose you found your brother in bed with your wife, and put a javelin through both of them, you would be justified.'

What happened next
Burton's account of his visit is regarded as the first balanced account of life at Salt Lake City (an earlier report was written by a lady who was outraged when some 'rude men' walked over a bridge before her), and he asserted that, for him, polygamy made sense in that time and place. He also received at least one proposal of marriage, which he declined. Back in England, he literally fell into the arms of Isabel Arundell, whom he had been courting, in defiance of her parents' displeasure, for many years. She wrote: 'He put his arm round my waist, and I put my head on his shoulder.' This was true love, as Burton looked awful, having suffered over 20 bad fever

attacks that had left his face a mess. When Burton died, Isabel buried him as a Catholic, to the dismay of his friends, and burned his erotic writings, to the dismay of erotomanes (she said she was acting under instruction from his spirit).

—59—

1863: JOHN WILKES BOOTH REFUSES TO MEET ABRAHAM LINCOLN

Abraham Lincoln enjoyed going to the theatre, and was a regular attender at Ford's Theatre in Washington after he became president in 1860. He was particularly fond of Shakespeare, but also derived much pleasure from popular melodramas. On 9 November 1863 he went to a performance of Charles Selby's *The Marble Heart*. The play was described by one London critic as 'a piece perilously elaborate in its development of sentiment and character, and ambitious in its aim as an Art-drama of the imaginative class'. The lead role was performed by John Wilkes Booth, brother of the great Shakespearian actor Edwin Booth.

Born into a prominent acting family, he was named 'John Wilkes' because of a supposed family connection to the English radical (☞ SEE 34), though he was much better looking than Wilkes, and had been billed as 'the handsomest man in America'. He was a strong believer in the institution of slavery, and had been briefly arrested in 1862 for his outspoken views.

In the course of the play, records Mary Clay, a member of Lincoln's party: 'Twice Booth in uttering disagreeable threats in the play came very near and put his finger close to Mr Lincoln's face; when he came a third time I was impressed by it, and said: "Mr Lincoln, he looks as if he meant that for you." "Well," he said, "he does look pretty sharp at me, doesn't he?"' Intrigued, the unflappable Lincoln sent a message backstage to Booth, inviting him to meet up with the president after the show. Booth refused.

1863 was a busy year for Lincoln. It began with his Emancipation Proclamation of 1 January, freeing all slaves in Confederate territory. Ten days after Booth's theatrical gestures, Lincoln gave his legendary speech dedicating the war cemetery at Gettysburg. Contemporary reaction to the Gettysburg Address was mixed, but it has come to be recognized as a rhetorical masterpiece: 'Four score and seven years ago our fathers brought forth on this continent, a new nation, conceived in Liberty, and dedicated to the proposition that all men are created equal.'

Lincoln, like Booth, was a great public speaker, but unlike Booth, when he wrote his own material he wrote it magnificently. If there are any great speeches by Booth or anyone else in defence of slavery, they remain unrecorded by posterity.

What happened next
If they had met backstage, would Booth still have found it possible to assassinate Lincoln (in the same theatre) in April 1865? The answer is probably yes. Booth was a good hater and just a year later was involved in a plot to kidnap the president, which could well have succeeded. With his brothers Edwin and Junius, he staged a performance of Julius Caesar to raise funds to erect a statue of Shakespeare (which is still there) in Central Park. When Booth finally assassinated Lincoln, he is supposed to have said *Sic semper tyrannis* (thus ever to tyrants), referring to Brutus's words after stabbing Caesar. Booth escaped Ford's theatre but was later killed by Union troops.

~60~

1864: GARIBALDI PLANTS A TREE FOR THE TENNYSONS

The Italian revolutionary Giuseppe Garibaldi was one of the most inspiring figures of the 19th century. A member of the Young Italy movement, he became the leading military figure of the Risorgimento, the post-1815 'resurgence' of Italian nationalism against foreign (mainly Austrian) occupation.

Garibaldi's mission had been immensely popular in Britain, and the government had even (covertly) aided his Sicilian campaign in 1860. He visited England in March 1864 to express his gratitude to the British people. Garibaldi fever was everywhere in Britain: the Russian exile Alexander Herzen described it as 'Carlyle's hero-worship being performed before our eyes'. Two rare dissenters were Queen Victoria, who described the reception as 'such follies', and Karl Marx, who called the Garibaldi craze 'a miserable spectacle of imbecility'.

But, generally, Garibaldi was greeted with great enthusiasm all round. On the one hand, the upper classes, led by various dukes and lords, invited him into their homes and to elaborate banquets, while on the other assorted progressives wanted him to speak at radical demonstrations.

Possibly in search of neutral ground, Garibaldi went to the Isle of Wight to visit the poet laureate, Alfred Lord Tennyson, who had written in praise of the great Italian hero. Tennyson was not disappointed when he met him: 'a noble human being'. Lady Tennyson also admired him greatly: 'A most striking figure in his picturesque white poncho lined with red, his embroidered red shirt and coloured tie over it. His face very noble, powerful, and sweet, his forehead high and square. Altogether he looked one of the great men of our Elizabethan age.'

Garibaldi planted a Wellingtonia tree in the Tennysons' garden (tree-planting had become one of his customs when visiting English people). Tennyson mentions the tree in his poem *To Ulysses*: 'Or watch the waving pine which here/ The warrior of Caprera set, / A name that earth will not forget/ Till earth has roll'd her latest year', and he records in a melancholy footnote characteristic of both men: 'Garibaldi said to me, alluding to his barren island, "I wish I had your trees".'

At the Tennysons, Garibaldi also met the great photographer Julia Margaret Cameron. Cameron – entering into the theatricality of the occasion – went down on her knees to ask Garibaldi for permission to take his portrait. Lady Tennyson was worried that Garibaldi might have thought Cameron was begging for money, but

Garibaldi, who was used to such tributes, accepted the gesture as it was intended (Cameron got her sitting).

What happened next
A whole range of products were branded 'Garibaldi' in Britain, from Garibaldi blouses to the still-popular Garibaldi biscuits. The emotional outpouring that greeted Garibaldi, uniting all classes (except for curmudgeons like Victoria and Marx), was unusual in Britain – one of the few comparable occasions perhaps being Princess Diana's death in 1997. The man himself engaged in a few more campaigns before retiring to his treeless island of Caprera, where he cultivated his fields until his death in 1882.

~ 61 ~

1871: WAGNER FAILS TO GET FUNDING FROM BISMARCK

It was to be expected that a meeting between Bismarck, recently victorious over France and now the chancellor of a united Germany, and Wagner, the most megalomaniacal of composers, would be a dramatic one, and so it was represented in many early biographies of Wagner. Wagnerians used to portray the meeting as one of two great Teutonic minds, who were not just creators of German culture and nationhood, but also purgers of non-German elements from the new Germany.

The encounter was really significant only for Wagner's truly monstrous ego. By 1871 the four operas of the *Ring Cycle* were mostly complete, and in that year Wagner was granted land by the Bayreuth town council to establish a regular Wagner festival in the town. Meanwhile, Bismarck had become chancellor of the newly unified Germany he had done so much to create, so this was hardly a meeting of equals (Wagner had actually sent Bismarck an embarrassing poem in his praise).

Wagner returned from the meeting and described it to his wife Cosima, who recorded in her diary that it had been a great success:

Richard had been very impressed by the humility of Bismarck, who observed to Wagner that all he had done in public life was 'obtain a few signatures'. They discussed art and politics. All was charm and sympathy, and the meeting was 'precious' to a satisfied Wagner, who for some reason refrained from asking for help with his great cultural project at Bayreuth. The diary entry, however, is suspect, and was amended at some later date – quite possibly by Wagner himself. Bismarck's own account of the meeting is a good deal less warm than Wagner's and the amendments may conceal a less-than-joyful first account. The tone of Bismarck's version of events is quite different: superior, even sarcastic. Bismarck wrote to a friend that Wagner seemed to expect a harmonious 'duet' to be played out, but went away disappointed, without even asking for money for Bayreuth.

What happened next
Under the Nazis, this meeting was seen as a pivotal moment in the history of German culture, but Bismarck's disdainful account most likely gives a truer picture of the meeting. As Wagner's biographer Hannu Salmi says, Bismarck had merely offhandedly 'offered a series of compliments which he himself regarded as insignificant mannerisms'. Wagner later wrote to Bismarck twice, in 1873 and 1875, offering him a splendid opportunity to aid the rebirth of the German spirit... by funding Wagner's operatic art. The Iron Chancellor did not reply.

～62～

1876: ROBERT INGERSOLL INSPIRES LEW WALLACE (THOUGH NOT AS HE INTENDED)

The crowded train heading towards the 1876 Indianapolis Republican Convention bore two renowned ex-soldiers: one was Robert Ingersoll, an evangelical atheist at least as famous in his day as Richard Dawkins is in ours, and the other was Lew Wallace, the man who was to become governor of New Mexico two years later (☛ SEE 63).

Ingersoll had served under Wallace in the American Civil War, as a colonel at the bloody battle of Shiloh, and later distinguished himself in mopping up Confederate guerrilla bands, before being captured. Wallace describes their chance encounter on the train in his preface to *The First Christmas* (1902). Ingersoll – a man who loved to converse anywhere and at any time – grabbed Wallace and said he felt like talking. Wallace said: '"Well, if you let me dictate the subject … I took seat by him, and began: "Is there a God?" Quick as a flash, he replied, "I don"t know: do you?" And then I – "Is there a Devil?" And he – "I don"t know: do you?" "Is there a Heaven?" "I don"t know, do you?" "Is there a Hell?" "I don"t know, do you?" "Is there a Hereafter?" "I don"t know, do you?" I finished, saying, "there, Colonel, you have the texts. Now go."'

And go Ingersoll did. He was one of the greatest orators of his day (an engraving depicts him in scary full flow at Walt Whitman's funeral), and here he was on his pet subject: the non-existence of God. Ingersoll spoke for two hours, only stopping when the train stopped. Says Wallace: 'He surpassed himself, and that is saying a great deal.'

Up until that point, Wallace's attitude to religion had been one of 'absolute indifference' but the weight of Ingersoll's rhetoric drove him to study religion and he ended up becoming a Christian. As he puts it, the result of listening to the great atheist was first, 'the book *Ben-Hur* and second, a conviction amounting to absolute belief in God and the Divinity of Christ'.

What happened next
In between dealing with dozens of bad hats as new Mexico governor, Wallace wrote *Ben-Hur: A Tale of the Christ,* which came out in 1880 and remains in print, one of the world's greatest bestsellers. It was the first work of fiction to be blessed by a pope, and has been filmed four times (it is not the bestselling American book ever, as is often claimed: *Gone With the Wind* outsold it in the 1930s). Robert Ingersoll died true to his atheist principles, despite the assertions of those who wish to claim him for agnosticism.

— 63 —

1879: LEW WALLACE PROMISES TO PARDON BILLY THE KID

Billy the Kid made his reputation in the Lincoln County Range War in New Mexico, which began in 1877 with the murder of an English rancher called John Tunstall (whose Colt revolver is displayed at the Royal Armouries Museum in Leeds). By the time the 'war' ended in 1881 around 20 men had been killed, some of them by Billy, who remarked that Tunstall 'was the only man that ever treated me like I was a free-born and white' and 'I'll get every son-of-a-bitch who helped kill John if it's the last thing I do'.

This 'war' encapsulates much of the dark side of American capitalism (with added cowboys). On one side was the firm of Murphy and Dolan, known as the 'House', merchants with lucrative monopoly contracts who supplied Indian reservations with beef. On the other was Tunstall, who ran a bank and merchant store, and had the backing of the cattle baron John Chisum (played by John Wayne as the incarnation of American individualism in the eponymous 1970 movie). Both sides used hired gunmen.

Two years into the conflict, the new governor, Lew Wallace (☞ SEE 62), drew up a list (which survives) of 36 men who should be arrested: Billy was 15th in a ranking headed by a merciless villain called John Selman. Wallace also declared an amnesty to be implemented if the person had not been indicted. Billy wrote to Wallace (this letter also survives) stating he was willing to surrender and also testify against selected murderers (Billy had signed a peace treaty with the 'House' killers), though he acknowledged that he was not eligible for the pardon.

Wallace wrote in reply saying that Billy could trust him: 'Come alone. Don't tell anybody – not a living soul – where you are coming or the object.' They then had a meeting to sort out the requisite ploys and testimonies. Wallace promised: 'I will let you go scot-free with a pardon in your pocket.' Billy agreed to a fake arrest, on the understanding that a pardon would be forthcoming, and was duly arrested and testified in court. Alas, no pardon came for Billy and he ended up simply walking out of jail and riding out of town. Billy's apologists say Wallace had no intention of pardoning him; others blame the district attorney; others say he just got bored. This was his first escape from the Lincoln County jail. In his second escape in 1881 (after writing three indignant letters to Wallace reminding him about the promised pardon) he killed two deputies.

What happened next
Wallace had been a distinguished soldier, and later became one of the bestselling novelists of the age – while governing his unruly domain, Wallace was writing *Ben-Hur* in his spare moments. One of the last official documents he signed was Billy's death warrant. The Kid was eventually shot by a former associate, Sheriff Pat Garrett, in 1881. In 1882, Garrett published a biography of Billy, depicting him as the iconic western desperado, which helped make him a legend. Garrett himself was murdered in obscure circumstances in 1908.

— 64 —

1882: OSCAR WILDE PERHAPS GETS A KISS FROM WALT WHITMAN

That Oscar Wilde's trip to America in 1882 was a success should not be a surprise. The aesthetic movement he embodied was then all the rage, and in any case, America has always loved big personalities, and Oscar was a *huge* personality.

His ship arrived in New York in January 1882 to a rapturous welcome perhaps not matched until the Beatles flew into New York in 1964. Reporters swarmed out in launches to meet Wilde's ship before it landed. Gilbert and Sullivan's opera *Patience,* with its satirical portrait of the Wildean aesthete Bunthorne, had been very popular in New York the previous year (at one surreal point on the tour he addressed an audience of flower-waving Harvard students all dressed as Bunthorne; Oscar had been tipped off, and trumped them by wearing sober evening dress). Oscar famously declared at

New York Customs 'I have nothing to declare except my genius' and in an interview said 'I am here to diffuse beauty, and I have no objection to saying that'.

A few weeks after arriving, Wilde went to visit Walt Whitman in Camden, New Jersey. He had described Whitman as one of his two favourite American poets (the other was Emerson). As has been pointed out, he possibly liked Poe better than either, but Poe was dead and so less useful for publicity purposes: Oscar was always a shrewd marketeer.

Wilde and Whitman gabbed away happily. Whitman was delighted to learn from Wilde that he and his friends had taken *Leaves of Grass* (Whitman's great 1855 poetry collection) on walks in Oxford. They shared a bottle of home-made elderberry wine and discussed Tennyson, Browning and Swinburne, as Whitman told the Philadelphia Press (poets were clearly big news in those far-distant days). They had 'a jolly good time' said Whitman, and Oscar was 'frank and outspoken and manly', without any affectation at all. For his part, Wilde later described Whitman as 'the grandest man I have ever seen'.

Leaves of Grass was still a controversial book in 1882. It was banned in Boston, causing sales to leap (of course). The criminologist George Ives, who campaigned for reform of the repressive laws on homosexuality, met Oscar in 1892, and records in a 1901 diary entry that when Wilde and Whitman parted, they exchanged a kiss; Ives says Oscar told him 'I have the kiss of Walt Whitman still on my lips'. Some have seen the kiss (of which Ives' diary entry is the only record) as a moment of awakening homosexual desire, but given that Oscar was 27 and Whitman 62, this seems doubtful.

What happened next
Two days later Wilde visited the novelist Henry James, but it was a less happy encounter. When James said he missed London, Oscar said (rather sniffily) 'You care for places? The world is my home', an inappropriate comment to the extremely cosmopolitan James. A fuming James decided that Wilde was 'a fatuous fool' and 'a tenth-rate cad' (James was not a man to provoke into insult). In

March, Oscar wrote to Whitman asking him to send a pamphlet for Swinburne, addressing him as 'My dear, dear Walt'.

— 65 —

1886: GERONIMO SURRENDERS TO GENERAL MILES

Apaches were long seen, in the popular, Hollywood-nurtured imagination, as short and sinister primitives. In fact, Apaches could be (a) huge, like the terrifying Mangas Colorado, or (b) ridiculously handsome, like the tasty army scout Peaches. Apaches are now more often seen as victims, but it has to be said that the memoirs of Apache life that we have, such as Jason Betzinez's *I Fought with Geronimo* (1959), portray a culture of remarkable violence. The Apaches were also riven by inter-clan feuding, and military expeditions always found Apache recruits eager to help attack rival bands.

Born around 1829, Geronimo's original name was Goyathlay, 'the Yawner'. The name 'Geronimo' is said to derive from frightened Mexicans invoking St Jerome when he attacked (his first wife and children were killed by Mexicans, and he was out for vengeance). Apache agent John Clum described him in his prime as 'erect as a mountain pine ... his stern features, his keen piercing eye, and his proud and graceful posture combined to create in him the model of an Apache war-chief'. By 1886, Geronimo had been fighting for about 40 years. He and his band of 30-odd warriors were being pursued by about 5,000 soldiers – a quarter of the American army. He sued for peace, and met General Crook under truce. Crook had a photographer with him, and the photographs of the event are the only known ones of Apaches truly dressed to kill.

Geronimo ran off and peace negotiations stalled. He finally surrendered to Crook's replacement, General Miles, with whom Geronimo had a cautiously staged encounter. Miles, says Geronimo, 'told me how we could be brothers to each other. We raised our hands to heaven and said that the treaty was not to be broken. We took an oath not to do any wrong to each other or to scheme against each other.' In truth, of course, neither trusted the other, and both were well aware this was the end game. Miles described Geronimo as having the 'clearest, sharpest, dark eye I think I have ever seen, unless it was that of General Sherman when he was at the prime of life ... Every movement indicated power, energy and determination. In everything he did he had a purpose.' Said Miles to the old warrior: 'I will take you under Government protection; I will build you a house ... I will give you cattle, horses, mules, and farming implements. You will be furnished with men to work the farm, for you yourself will not have to work ... If you agree to this treaty you shall see your family within five days.' Geronimo's response was blunt: 'sounds like a story to me'.

What happened next
Geronimo was a dreadful whinger, always complaining even when he was clearly in the wrong, but the subsequent treatment of his band was very poor. They were deported to Florida and eventually ended up in Fort Sill, Oklahoma. Geronimo became much in demand at fairs, where he sold his autograph. Geronimo died in 1909 after a drunken fall. For collectors of intriguing names, he had a son called Robbie, a brother called Fatty, and a warrior called Fun (who shot himself).

— **66** —

1887: QUEEN VICTORIA MEETS BLACK ELK

'Buffalo Bill' Cody first brought his Wild West show to Britain in 1887, in Queen Victoria's Jubilee Year. The show was a huge success, and Cody returned in 1891-92 (drawing £10,000 in revenue in Cardiff alone), and again in 1902 and 1904.

The snootiest comment on the show's reception in Britain actually came from an American, the poet James Russell Lowell, who attributed its success to 'the dullness of the average English mind'. If so, it was a dullness shared by Queen Victoria, who was entranced by the Indians, in particular by the Lakota, who in turn revered her as

'Grandmother England'. For them, Canada was the grandmother's country, a place of sanctuary patrolled by her soldiers, who wore red coats so they could see them and know they were safe from the US Cavalry. When Sitting Bull (who later toured occasionally with Cody's show in the USA) had taken his people across the border into Canada in 1877, he showed a Mountie a medal given to an ancestor by the British for help in fighting the rebellious Americans. For the Lakota, the British were old friends.

In 1905, during vicious divorce proceedings, Cody's wife Lulu alleged that Victoria had made improper advances to Cody during this English trip. Even in old age Cody was a fine-looking man, but this remarkable allegation is unfounded. All observers agreed that Victoria was most impressed by the Lakota, especially (as testified in her diary) the handsome Red Shirt.

The 1891 tour included a ceremony in Manchester to honour special guests, the 19 surviving members of the famous 'Charge of the Light Brigade' at the Battle of Balaclava in 1854. Also present, though not highlighted, were another 19 survivors: Lakota who had survived the previous year's massacre of their kin by the 7th Cavalry at Wounded Knee. They included Black Elk, who, at the age of 12, had ridden beside his cousin Crazy Horse at the Battle of the Little Bighorn in 1876. He would later recall that after inviting the Lakota to Windsor, Victoria told him that if they were her subjects, she 'would not let them take you around in a show like this'.

What happened next
Victoria's beloved husband Prince Albert had died in 1862, and Victoria had gone into a long period of mourning that eventually affected the popularity of the monarchy. Even *The Times,* that voice of the establishment, suggested that it might now be time for the country to consider becoming a republic. Victoria remained a virtual recluse from the nation for many years, and few entertainments were requested by the woman Kipling called the 'Widow at Windsor'. Consequently, when Victoria announced she would attend Cody's show at Earl's Court there was great excitement. The popularity of the monarchy soared and talk of a republic receded. As for Black Elk, he lived until 1950, a revered medicine man and an acknowledged

spokesmen for all Native Americans. His memoir, *Black Elk Speaks*, is regarded by many as a founding text of New Age thinking, but despite that doubtful accolade it remains an inspirational text.

—67—

1889: NELLIE BLY CHARMS JULES VERNE

Elizabeth Jane Cochran was born in 1864 in Pennsylvania. Her father, a judge, died when she was 4, leaving a financial mess. Aged 18, she read a piece in the *Pittsburgh Dispatch* saying that women should keep to their 'proper sphere'. She wrote a protest letter to the editor which so impressed him, that he commissioned a second piece and hired her. She adopted the pen name 'Nellie Bly' (derived from a Stephen Foster song).

Nellie proved to be not just a good writer but a brave investigative reporter, and at one point was thrown out of Mexico for exposing corruption. In 1887 she was recruited by Joseph Pulitzer for the *New York World*, where she pushed the limits of what was acceptable for women reporters by getting herself committed to a lunatic asylum to expose its horrors.

In November 1889, in a stunt inspired by Jules Verne's *Around the World in 80 Days* (1872), she set off from New York to travel around the world within 80 days, with two small cases, a reliable timepiece and some good flannel underwear. While in France she took a detour to meet Verne. They met in Amiens, with a translator (and Madame Verne) in attendance.

Verne was amazed at how young Nellie was and asked about her route. She said: 'My line of travel is from New York to London, then Calais, Brindisi, Port Said, Ismailia, Suez, Aden, Colombo, Penang, Singapore, Hong Kong, Yokohama, San Francisco, New York.'

Verne asked why not visit Bombay, as Phileas Fogg had done: 'Because I am more anxious to save time than a young widow,' she answered, referring to one of Fogg's adventures. 'You may save a young widower before you return,' replied a smiling Verne.

Then Nellie records that Verne's wife 'put up her pretty face' for a kiss. 'I stifled a strong inclination to kiss her on the lips, they were so sweet and red, and show her how we do it in America. My mischievousness often plays havoc with my dignity, but for once I was able to restrain myself, and kissed her softly after her own fashion.' Said Nellie: 'I had travelled many miles out of my way for the privilege of meeting M. and Mme. Verne, and I felt that if I had gone around the world for that pleasure, I should not have considered the price too high.'

What happened next
Nellie actually completed the trip in 72 days, 6 hours and 11 minutes, truly a world record, and when she arrived back in New York she had become probably the most famous woman in the world. She was greeted with fireworks and brass bands, though not with the financial bonus she reasonably expected from her employer. Nellie's experiences on her voyage had appeared daily in the *World* and were followed eagerly by people around the world as well as America. Nellie resigned in indignation, but returned to the *World* in 1893, and became a leading instigator of reform, exposing sweatshop oppression of women and the struggles of unmarried mothers. She died in 1922, mourned by many whose lives she had helped change for the better.

— 68 —

1890: JOSEPH CONRAD AND ROGER CASEMENT SHARE A ROOM...

... for 10 days, which is a bit longer than many of our other brief encounters, but they were very busy men and did not spend much time together – and for some of the time Casement was away escorting 'a large lot of ivory'.

The Dublin-born Casement began working for colonial enterprises in the Congo in 1884, beginning with the Belgian King Leopold's International Association, and by 1890 he was operating a trading station at the port of Matadi. The Polish-born Conrad had become a British national in 1886, the year he gained his master's certificate. By 1890 he was an experienced seaman, and had been shipwrecked in Sumatra. Conrad was tough, and had survived shooting himself in the chest at the age of 21, in a failed suicide attempt.

Conrad and Casement liked each other. Conrad wrote in his diary: 'Made the acquaintance of Mr Roger Casement, which I should consider as a great pleasure under any circumstances and now it becomes a positive piece of luck. Thinks, speaks well, most intelligent and very sympathetic.' In the next few words, Conrad speaks of avoiding whites 'as much as possible', but this is no reflection on Casement. Casement described Conrad to a friend as 'a charming man … subtle, kind and sympathetic'.

The year they met was also the year that Conrad served as mate on a Congo steamer, a voyage that resulted years later in *Heart of Darkness* (1899), the novel which inspired the nightmare river journey in the Vietnam movie *Apocalypse Now* (1979).

What happened next
The two men later corresponded and briefly met once more, in 1903, when Casement had a 'delightful day' at Conrad's home near Hythe. By then Conrad was one of Britain's leading writers, while Casement was a career diplomat. Casement's damning report into the horrors of Belgian administration in the Congo was published the following year in 1904. During World War I, Casement embraced the armed struggle for an Irish Republic, and helped prepare for the 1916 Easter Rising in Dublin. He tried to recruit Irish POWs in Germany to fight the British; only a very few signed up and a chastened Casement returned to Ireland, convinced the Rebellion would fail. He landed by German submarine, was captured and eventually executed for treason in 1916. Conrad strongly disapproved of what he regarded as Casement's treachery, but also wrote: 'I judged that he was a man, properly speaking, of no mind at all. I don't mean stupid. I mean that he was all emotion … A creature of sheer temperament – a truly tragic personality.'

From ONE WORLD WAR *to* ANOTHER (20th CENTURY *to* 1945)

~ 69 ~

1900: WINSTON CHURCHILL MEETS WINSTON S CHURCHILL

While still in his mid-twenties, Winston Churchill took part in the last British cavalry charge, at the Battle of Omdurman in 1898 (though a war correspondent, he rode with the Lancers), escaped from a Boer prison camp in 1899, and was elected Tory MP for Oldham in 1900 (at the second attempt). Instead of going to the opening of Parliament, however, Churchill took himself off on a speaking tour of Britain and the USA. He needed money, and his agent promised that the tour would earn him over £10,000 in a month (not an improbable figure – he had already earned over £4,000 that year speaking in England). He landed in America in December 1900.

He received a mixed welcome. He was drolly introduced by Mark Twain in New York thus: 'Mr Churchill by his father is an Englishman, by his mother he is an American, no doubt a blend that makes a perfect man', but he was heckled at many events by those outraged at Britain's perceived oppression of the Boers (and the Irish).

Incredible though it may seem, there was another Winston Churchill doing the rounds: Winston Churchill the 29-year-old author of the current bestselling historical novel *Richard Carvel* (1899). The two men, alert to the possibility of confusion in the book trade, had already corresponded. (Half-)British Winston had written to wholly American Winston thus: 'Mr Winston Churchill presents his compliments to Mr Winston Churchill and begs to draw his attention to a matter which concerns them both.' He suggested that in future he would sign his books 'Winston S Churchill' thus happily settling the matter.

They finally met in Boston, inevitably being introduced: 'Mr Churchill, Mr Churchill.' They had dinner, and discussed American Winston's new novel *The Crisis* (not to be confused with Winston S's later *The World Crisis of* 1923-31). Winston S felt there was not enough warfare in *The Crisis* for a novel about the American Civil War: 'put more fighting in it', he said. A *Boston Herald* reporter asked him how he was getting on with his namesake: 'We have become very good friends,' he replied.

What happened next
British Winston asked his new friend: 'Why don't you go into politics? I mean to be Prime Minister of Britain. It would be a great lark if you were President of the United States at the same time.' American Winston did in fact became a member of the New Hampshire legislature and even ran for governor, but his political career never took off. None of his novels are now in print.

— 70 —

1906: MARK TWAIN MEETS RUSSIAN REVOLUTIONARY MAXIM GORKY

When the two great writers Maxim Gorky and Mark Twain met on 11 April 1906, they inspired a striking headline in *The New York Times*: GORKY AND TWAIN PLEAD FOR REVOLUTION. Gorky had been sent into internal exile in Russia for his political beliefs, and was now a prominent member of Lenin's faction within the Social Democratic Party (soon to become famous as the 'Bolsheviks'), on whose behalf he travelled to the USA to raise funds.

What was called an 'American auxiliary movement' to bring about freedom in Russia was launched at a 5th Avenue dinner in honour of Gorky, at which Gorky himself and Twain were the principal speakers. Said Twain: 'Let us hope that fighting will be postponed or averted for a while, but if it must come I am most emphatically in sympathy with the movement now on foot in Russia to make that country free.' Responded Gorky: 'Mark Twain ... is a man of force. He has always impressed me as a blacksmith who stands at his anvil with the fire burning and strikes hard and hits the mark every time. I come to America expecting to find true and warm sympathizers among the American people ... Now is the time for the revolution. Now is the time for the overthrow of Czardom. Now! Now! Now!

But we need the sinews of war, the blood we will give ourselves. We need money, money, money. I come to you as a beggar that Russia may be free.'

New York's rich and poor eagerly donated to the Bolshevik cause, but this unlikely idyll of Russo-American friendship quickly ran aground on the rock of American propriety. *The New York Times* asked Mrs Gorky if she had acted in her husband's plays. 'Long ago,' she replied. 'At present I am just my husband's wife, nothing else, and I don't wish to be before the public in any other capacity.' But the American public was shocked to discover that the Gorkys were not legally married. Though they were married by Russian custom, that was not good enough for New York hotels. As Twain's patrician friend William Dean Howells noted (from a lofty height): 'The next day Gorky was expelled from his hotel with the woman who was not his wife, but who, I am bound to say, did not look as if she were not, at least to me, who am, however, not versed in those aspects of human nature.' All talk of the Russian Revolution evaporated in the heat of what was called the 'domestic interest' of the situation.

What happened next
A few days later came news of the San Francisco earthquake, and scandalized reports on the Gorkys ceased as the papers filled with news of the disaster. Gorky spent the next seven years in comfortable exile (mostly in a Capri villa). He took literary revenge on New York in his story entitled 'The City of the Yellow Devil'.

～71～

1910: SIR ARNOLD BAX IMPRESSES PATRICK PEARSE WITH HIS LOVE OF CELTIC TWILIGHT

Dublin at the start of the 20th century was a culturally vibrant city. The greatest novel of the 20th century, Joyce's *Ulysses*, would take the city (as it was on 16 June 1904) as its setting, though it would be published in Paris in 1922 (☛ SEE 77).

Joyce's earthy Dublin, however, was not the only literary version of Ireland. There was also the popular world of Celtic myth, turned into a cultural phenomenon which took its name from Yeats's story collection, *The Celtic Twilight* (1893). Young romantics such as the English composer Arnold Bax were enraptured by all things 'Celtic', and Bax was later described by one Russian critic as 'the Celtic voice in English music'. In 1902 he toured Ireland with his brother and wrote fey prose and poetry of the sort indistinguishable from that produced by hundreds of other pale young men and women throughout Britain and Ireland. Much of what we think of as 'Celtic' was actually invented during this period, even, indeed, the name 'Fiona', which was the brainchild of one of those poets, Fiona Macleod (who was actually a man, William Sharp, who donned a nice frock to write Celtic poetry).

Bax wrote under the name of 'Dermot O'Byrne' (he later called his children Dermot and Maeve), and settled in Dublin, where one of his neighbours was the poet 'AE', George Russell. In the manner of the era, Russell hosted a salon in his house, where, every Sunday, intellectuals could gather and chat. Many of the guests were prominent nationalists. One evening when Bax was present, he met Patrick Pearse. Bax was fascinated by Pearse, who had recently edited the Gaelic League's newspaper, and had been doing sterling work for years in spreading Gaelic culture and education. Pearse and the young Englishman had a shared love of Ireland's west country, and when Bax left, Pearse told another guest: 'I think your friend Arnold Bax may be one of us. I should like to see more of him.'

By 'one of us' Pearse meant someone for whom Gaelic culture was tied into Irish nationalism. For Pearse, as for many other nationalists of the time, Irish mythological heroes such as Cuchulainn were figures to inspire heroic acts, and religion was also added to this potent mixture: Pearse regarded Christ's sacrifice and redemption as an example (he would have loved Mel Gibson's movies). As Ruth Dudley Edwards said, Pearse's heroes 'died painful deaths'. Yeats said of him: 'a dangerous man; he has the vertigo of self-sacrifice.'

What happened next
In 1913, Pearse became a co-founder of the Irish Volunteers, a paramilitary organization founded in response to the anti-Home Rule Ulster Volunteers. He was one of the leaders of the Easter Rising against British rule in 1916, and was executed in its aftermath. He is still regarded by many in the way he wanted – as a revolutionary martyr. Bax later described Pearse as 'leader of Ireland for a week'. Bax accepted a knighthood in 1937 (with mixed feelings) and became Master of the King's Musick in 1942. One of his last works was a Coronation March for Elizabeth II.

─72─

1914: GAVRILO PRINCIP SHOOTS FRANZ FERDINAND AND HIS DUCHESS (AND STARTS WORLD WAR I)

In one of Geoffrey Household's short stories, a man recollects how he inadvertently caused World War I by directing the assassin Gavrilo Princip to the exact spot where he was able to shoot Archduke Franz Ferdinand (and his duchess Sophie) on that June day that changed the world forever. The assassination did indeed only happen through fortuitous (as it were) circumstances. Princip was 19 years old, ill with tuberculosis and devoted to the cause of Serb nationalism. He belonged to 'Young Bosnia,' a group of Serbs dedicated to the overthrow of the Austro-Hungarian Empire's rule in the Balkans, and received training in the dark arts of sabotage and murder from the Serb secret society popularly known as the 'Black Hand' (also called, more bluntly, 'Union or Death'), which provided the ordnance for the deed.

Franz Ferdinand, in his capacity as inspector general of the imperial army, paid an official visit to Sarajevo, and arrived at the railway station at 10am on 28 June. This was St Vitus' Day, sacred to many Serbs, as exactly 525 years previously the Serbs had suffered a catastrophic defeat at the hands of the Ottomans at the Battle of Kosovo. The symbolic importance of the day contributed to the resolve of a bunch of would-be assassins waiting for Ferdinand, consisting of Princip and five others. When Ferdinand's motorcade passed, one of the gang threw a fizzing bomb that Ferdinand actually warded off with his arm, and which went under the car following before exploding. The injured were taken to hospital.

Ferdinand and his group arrived at Sarajevo town hall and debated what to do next. Amazingly, Ferdinand – after trying to persuade his wife not to go along – decided they should go back along the same route and visit the hospital where the wounded were being treated (there is a photograph of them entering the car for the return journey). On the way back – for reasons that are still unclear – Ferdinand's chauffeur took a wrong turning and managed to stop just beside a surprised Princip, who pulled out his pistol and shot first Sophie and then Ferdinand, his two bullets severing arteries in both victims (as ill luck would have it, Ferdinand's bodyguard was on the other side of the car). Ferdinand called to Sophie, 'Don't die! Live for our children', and said 'It is nothing' when asked if he was in pain. They died within minutes.

What happened next
At his trial, Princip denied wanting to shoot Sophie. Her killing was an 'accident'. He was too young to execute, and was sentenced to 20 years in jail. Austria-Hungary declared war on Serbia on 28 July, which led to a complex network of treaties being invoked, thus beginning World War I. Princip became a hero to many Serbs, and his pistol shots set off a war in which perhaps as many as 19 million people died before its end in November 1918. Princip died of his tuberculosis earlier that year, in April.

～73～

1914: PANCHO VILLA SHARES A PHOTO OPPORTUNITY WITH EMILIANO ZAPATA

The decade-long Mexican Revolution of 1910-20 was bloody, with death toll estimates ranging from one to two million. Several revolutionary leaders were assassinated, including the two everyone has heard of, Zapata and Villa.

Pancho Villa's fearsome military abilities took him from banditry and cattle rustling to become a major revolutionary figure in a few short years. He was an extraordinarily media-savvy revolutionary, and is certainly the first to have signed exclusive contracts with a movie company. He is even said to have delayed a battle until the newsreel cameras got into position.

The other great peasant revolutionary, the ex-sharecropper Emiliano Zapata, was as committed to the revolution as Villa, but less concerned with killing people than with setting up redistribution commissions and implementing his scheme for land reform, the 'Plan de Ayala'.

Villa's forces were based in the north, while Zapata's Liberation Army was fighting in the south, so they closed in on the lands in between, which were controlled by the Federales, commanded by unpredictable and often highly brutal generals.

The two men finally met on 4 December 1914, on the outskirts of Mexico City, and agreed to an alliance prior to occupying the city. Villa, always alert to a good photo opportunity, posed with Zapata in a frequently reproduced photograph taken in the National Palace. The photograph shows Villa sitting on the presidential throne – Zapata declined the opportunity – beaming off-camera to his right while inclining slightly to his left, towards where Zapata is sitting. Zapata has his sombrero on his knee (one of several splendid hats in the picture) and the two men are surrounded by their followers, whose features range from Indian to Spanish, and who look like a mixed bag of cut-throats, intellectuals and excitement-seekers – which is exactly what they were, the raw material of many a revolution.

What happened next
Villa and Zapata formed a loose alliance against the constitutionalist politician Carranza, whom they accused of seeking to become dictator (Carranza was elected president in 1915 and would be assassinated in 1920). Villa – whose troops were not as disciplined as Zapata's – was obliged to leave Mexico City early in 1915, eventually retiring (more or less) in 1920. He was murdered in 1923. Though

Zapata was assassinated in 1919, he continues to inspire rebellion. At the end of the 20th century a 'Zapatista Army of National Liberation' established control of part of the southern Mexican state of Chiapas, in direct defiance of the North American Free Trade Agreement.

— 74 —

1918: FANNY KAPLAN SHOOTS LENIN

Though she is famous as the woman who almost killed Lenin, much of what we know about Fanny Kaplan remains uncertain – even her first name. She may have been born Vera, and was also known as Dora. She may also have had some connection with the British Secret Service spy Sidney Reilly – the legendary 'Ace of Spies', who was himself Russian-born, and even more of an enigma – but the early 20th-century revolutionary waters she inhabited were murky indeed. Speculation apart, however, Fanny's political background shows her to be a classic revolutionary of her time and place. Born in 1883 into a peasant family, she was Jewish at a time when there were severe restrictions on Jews in Russia, and when Jewish activists operated at every level of resistance.

Fanny joined the Socialist Revolutionary Party and was wounded in 1906 when transporting explosives in Kiev – the explosives were to be used to blow up a tsarist official. She was deported to Siberia, where she languished in ill health for 11 years, only being released after the February Revolution of 1917, which established a Constituent Assembly. In October the Bolsheviks seized power, and in January 1918, to the amazement of Russian progressives (the more naive ones, at least), the assembly that Russians had struggled and died for over the course of many decades of great sacrifice was simply dissolved by Bolshevik diktat.

In August 1918, Fanny accosted Lenin in the street. She challenged him briefly about the Bolshevik tyranny, then shot at him three times, hitting him twice. Under interrogation, Fanny expressed no remorse and said that Lenin had betrayed the Revolution by dissolving the Constituent Assembly.

What happened next

Fanny Kaplan was shot in September and her body was ordered to be destroyed, 'without trace'. The assassination attempt gives rise to one of the great 'what ifs' of history. The death of Lenin might well have led to the end of the Bolsheviks' grip on power, in which Lenin's personal rule was such a decisive factor. Lenin died in 1924, with one of Fanny's bullets still in his neck. By this date, the Revolution's power structures – most particularly the Cheka, the organization which dealt ruthlessly with perceived subversion – were firmly in place. At the time of Fanny's execution, the Red Army's newspaper called for the shedding of 'floods' of bourgeois blood, and in the immediate aftermath of the execution, thousands more – many of them old socialists – were murdered during what became known as the Red Terror. During the Civil War period of 1918-21, tens of thousands of 'state enemies' were to be summarily executed. Millions more were to die in the famines and purges of the 1920s and 1930s.

— 75 —

1920: LENIN DISAPPOINTS BERTRAND RUSSELL

It is said that T S Eliot was once told by a London taxi driver: 'Only the other evening I picked up Bertrand Russell, and I said to him: "Well, Lord Russell, what's it all about?", and, do you know, he couldn't tell me'. Despite the disappointment, the anecdote illustrates how Russell became not only the most famous living philosopher, but, for many, a man who was expected to know everything.

In 1920, Russell travelled to Russia as part of a 'fact-finding' trade delegation. Russell was a leading pacifist and socialist, but he found little to praise in the communist experiment taking place in Russia. He met a 'heartbroken' Gorky (☛ SEE 70), who was backing the Bolsheviks because he feared what might replace them; he begged Russell to keep in mind while making his judgement 'what Russia has suffered'.

Russell also met Lenin. In his autobiography, Russell records that he found Lenin 'disappointing' and glimpsed an 'impish cruelty' in the man. Later, he was to go further, and told broadcaster Alistair Cooke that he believed Lenin was the most evil man he ever met: 'He had steady black eyes that never flickered. I hoped to make them flicker at one point by asking him why it was thought necessary to murder hundreds of thousands of kulaks. He quite calmly ignored the word "murder". He smiled and said they were a nuisance that stood in the way of his agricultural plans.'

Many other socialists came to Soviet Russia from the 1920s to the early 1980s, prepared to see a workers' paradise and often went away convinced they had found it. Russell described such views as a 'tragic delusion', and set out his comments in *The Practice and Theory of Bolshevism* (1921). It is typical of Russell's intellectual honesty that, though he knew the book would be welcomed by his political opponents in Britain and would cause offence to fellow socialists, he published it anyway. Said Russell: 'The time I spent in Russia was one of increasing nightmare. Cruelty, poverty, suspicion, persecution, formed the very air we breathed.' There was a veneer of equality, and everybody was called 'tovarish', but as Russell pointed out, 'comrade' meant one thing when addressed to a peasant, another when addressed to Lenin.

What happened next
Other British socialists visited Lenin, including H G Wells, who described Lenin as a man who laughed a lot, but whose laugh was 'grim'. Russia was a despotic regime, concluded Wells. Trotsky described Wells as 'condescending' and (the inevitable insult) 'bourgeois', but Wells and Russell are still read, and the USSR is now long gone.

— 76 —

1922: W E JOHNS ENLISTS AIRCRAFTMAN ROSS (LAWRENCE OF ARABIA)

WE Johns was the creator of the pilot Biggles, one of the most popular figures in children's fiction. Biggles is hero of no fewer than 102 books, starting off in World War I biplanes and ending up flying jets in the 1960s. Johns himself fought at Gallipoli in 1915, aged 22. He transferred to the Royal Flying Corps in 1917, and while training wrote off three aircraft in three days, through no fault of his own (it has been suggested that Johns may have destroyed ten British aircraft in training, which would have qualified him as a German 'Ace').

He became a bomber pilot in what is now the Royal Air Force in July 1918, and was shot down in September. His observer was killed and Johns, who somehow survived his goggles being shot to pieces, was wounded in the leg, and only narrowly escaped execution by a German firing squad. After the November Armistice, he returned to his family – who had believed him dead – on Christmas Day.

Johns became an RAF recruiting officer, and in 1922, in the Covent Garden office, interviewed a man called John Hume Ross who wanted to enlist as a mechanic. Johns quickly decided Ross was a 'suspicious character'. He was in poor health, had no identification or references, and was clearly using an assumed name. Johns rejected him. 'Ross', however, was actually one of the most famous men in the world: T E Lawrence, or 'Lawrence of Arabia'. Lawrence, tired of his fame, wanted to hide away in the RAF. It was formerly assumed that Lawrence managed to fool everyone when enlisting, but in fact he cleared things with Air Marshal Sir Hugh Trenchard, asking to enlist 'in the ranks, of course… the newspapers used to run after me and I like being private'. Trenchard agreed, but wondered 'whether it could be kept secret'.

When Lawrence arrived to sign up, he was supposed to be met by a chap called Dexter, who was to sign him up 'no questions asked'.

Unfortunately, he got Johns, whose rejection was quickly overruled. A message arrived, signed, says Johns, by 'a very high authority', ordering his enlistment. Thus Lawrence of Arabia became John Hume Ross, Aircraftman Second Class (A/C2) No.352087.

What happened next
As Trenchard guessed, the newspapers found out. Lawrence was discharged, then re-enlisted in the tank corps as T E Shaw. He lasted two years, then got back into the RAF after threatening to kill himself. At every stage he was helped by his many admirers, ranging from the socialist George Bernard Shaw to old imperialists such as John Buchan. Lawrence left the RAF in 1935, and was killed a few weeks later in a motorcycle crash. Johns became a hugely successful novelist, whose work is both more realistic and less reactionary than is often assumed. Biggles, for example, speaks Hindi and despises racism. In 1940, Johns also created a heroine, Worrals of the WAAF, a female equivalent of Biggles who takes no sexist nonsense from men, and features in eleven novels.

―77―

1922: PROUST, JOYCE, DIAGHILEV, STRAVINSKY AND PICASSO SHARE A NIGHT AT THE MAJESTIC

In 1922 the English novelist Sydney Schiff (who wrote under the name of Stephen Hudson) had one of the best cultural ideas of his time: he and his wife would host a party to which they would invite the leading cultural figures of the day. Richard Davenport-Hines, whose book *A Night At the Majestic: Proust & the Great Modernist Dinner Party of 1922* (2006) is the definitive guide to the occasion, describes the Schiffs as 'the first celebrity stalkers'. The French novelist Marcel Proust was the main target, and Schiff rather bizarrely described him as the 'only man I like and I don't intend to like any other'.

Schiff was wealthy, cosmopolitan and well-connected: the party was arranged for the Majestic Hotel, Paris, 18 May 1922 (Schiff had wanted the Ritz, but the Ritz banned music after midnight). Schiff seized the opportunity presented by the première that evening of Stravinsky's ballet *Le Renard,* performed by Diaghilev's Ballets Russes, in order to stage the gathering. Among those invited, apart from Proust, were the Paris-based Irish writer James Joyce, Russian impresario Serge Diaghilev, Russian composer Igor Stravinsky and Spanish artist Pablo Picasso.

The Schiffs were anxious to see if their 'lions' would all appear. Diaghilev had made sure of his Ballets Russes colleagues Picasso and Stravinsky, but Joyce and Proust were notoriously unreliable and were not present for the dinner. Joyce arrived in time for the coffee, apologized to the Schiffs for being late and also for having no formal clothes. The Schiffs didn't care: Joyce's novel *Ulysses* had been published two months earlier in Paris, and rumours about its greatness were abundant. He could have come in dungarees, for all the Schiffs cared, though they would have doubtless preferred him sober, which he certainly was not.

An immaculately dressed Proust rolled in about 2.30am. He had once been known as 'Proust of the Ritz', but, if not quite a total recluse now, his gadabout days were long gone. Proust and Stravinsky began to chat, at which point a princess, annoyed by rumours that one of Proust's characters was based on her, flounced out of the room. Flustered, Proust asked Stravinsky if he liked Beethoven. 'I detest Beethoven,' said an irritated Stravinsky, and at this point Joyce (who had lost consciousness) began to snore loudly.

Joyce (when he woke up) attached himself to his fellow writer for the rest of the proceedings, but as Proust's biographer William Carter says, 'the creators of Leopold Bloom and Charles Swann had little to say to each other'. Later, Joyce would tell a friend that he didn't rate Proust: 'I have read some pages of his. I cannot see any special talent but I am a bad critic.' Joyce's later versions of the encounter vary a lot; Proust never spoke of it. Picasso – sadly but perhaps wisely – doesn't seem to have mingled much that evening.

What happened next
Schiff later tried to persuade Proust to sit for Picasso, but with no success. Proust had only six months to live, and the time was possibly

shortened when at the end of the party Joyce jumped into a taxi with the Schiffs and Proust, and started smoking. Proust, who somehow managed to be allergic to both smoke *and* fresh air, did not invite Joyce up to his apartment for a nightcap. The party was over.

─ 78 ─

1923: THOMAS HARDY ENTERTAINS THE PRINCE OF WALES (BUT NOT VERY MUCH)

Born in 1840, the young Thomas Hardy watched public executions in Dorchester, and lived to write verses about Einstein in the 1920s. However, in the course of this long life filled with many remarkable encounters, perhaps the oddest happened in July 1923.

In 1923 Hardy was a bestselling and critically well-regarded novelist and something of a national institution. He corresponded with young guns such as Ezra Pound and was visited by Lawrence of Arabia. Then 82, he had begun to study Einstein and noted, in June 1923: 'Relativity. That things and events always were, are, and will be.' He already believed that necessity governed the universe, not chance. While Edward, Prince of Wales was visiting the English West Country, says Hardy's biographer Claire Tomalin, someone in Edward's entourage, whether through necessity or chance remains unknown, came up with 'the bright idea that the visit might be more entertaining' if the prince had lunch at Thomas Hardy's house in Dorset.

Florence, Hardy's wife, found the idea of entertaining the prince and his retinue fairly scary, but Hardy was blasé about the whole thing, suggesting to his sister Kate that she could hide in 'the bedroom behind the jessamine – you would then see him come, and go: we could probably send you up a snack'. Edward said to Hardy: 'My mother tells me you have written a book called *Tess of the d'Urbervilles*. I must try to read it some time.' Edward had somehow failed to inherit his great-grandmother Victoria's ability to be at ease with people from very different backgrounds (☞ SEE 66). Edward was a royal who had not yet become a gentleman. Also, he was not a reader; when given a copy of *Wuthering Heights*, he said: 'Who is this woman Brunt?'

Edward ascended with his valet to a bedroom and Florence looked out of a window in time to see a scrunched up waistcoat fly out of the bedroom. They all had lunch together (Edward waistcoat-less) under the trees, and everything went quite well – as Tomalin says, someone had the good sense to lock up the Hardys' bad-tempered terrier.

The encounter amused many contemporaries, and inspired a neat little Max Beerbohm poem in the Hardy style: 'A Luncheon': '... Yes, Sir, I've written several books ...\ We are both of us aged by our strange brief nighness \But each of us lives to tell the tale. \Farewell, farewell, Your Royal Highness.'

What happened next
The next day, the Hardys motored over to visit a very different companion, the great apostle of birth control Marie Stopes. Hardy died in 1928, mourned by a nation. Edward became Edward VIII but abdicated his throne in 1936 for love of Wallis Simpson. He then became the Duke of Windsor, and possibly also less of a philistine, but sadly there was no one left to pick his company for him except Wallis.

☛ SEE ALSO **83) 1937: *The Duke of Windsor meets (and salutes) Hitler.***

━79━

1927: THE EINSTEINS VISIT THE FREUDS

By 1927 Albert Einstein and Sigmund Freud were both household names, the pinnacles of the powerful Jewish element in German-speaking culture: Freud, aged 70, was the world's leading psychologist, Einstein (a sprightly 47) was the world's leading physicist, indeed probably its most famous scientist of any kind. At the end of 1926 Albert and Elsa Einstein, who lived in Berlin, heard that the Vienna-based Sigmund and Martha Freud were to visit family in the city, and arranged to call on them in the New Year.

The Einsteins stayed for two hours. Freud said afterwards to a friend that he and Einstein had a very pleasant chat together, though their fields of study were mutually incomprehensible; Einstein, said Freud, understood as much about psychology as he in turn understood about physics.

For Einstein, in fact, psychoanalysis just didn't make sense, and he didn't see how it could be useful. Not long after the meeting, a friend suggested to Einstein that analysis might be useful for him, and Einstein responded with 'regret' that he would not be taking up the suggestion as he would like to remain in the 'darkness' of having never been psychoanalysed. Einstein's own son, Eduard, was mentally ill, and he and Elsa seem never to have even considered the possibility of seeking advice from Freud. Einstein told a friend that he had no need for help from the 'medical side' for Eduard's condition and judged it best to 'let nature run its course'. Freud himself had a son, Oliver (named after Oliver Cromwell), whom he diagnosed as having 'obsessional neurosis'. Who knows what he would have made of Eduard Einstein?

What happened next

The two remained in contact after their 1927 meeting. In 1932, when the League of Nations asked Einstein to pick a partner with whom to reflect on a great issue of the day, Einstein choose as his question 'Is there any way of delivering mankind from the menace of war?', and as his partner he chose Freud. Freud's response surprised everyone by being quite cheering: we are aggressive so we hunger for war, but we also love, so we want peace – and peace would win out in the end. Einstein looked to international action and laws to solve the war problem. The discussion resulted in a book called *Why War?*, published in 1932 by the League of Nations. Uninfluenced by Freud's optimism, the Nazis came to power in 1933, and the book was one of many publicly burned in the streets of Berlin. Einstein left Germany for Princeton University in the USA in 1933, while Freud would leave Vienna for London following the Nazi annexation of Austria in 1938.

☛ SEE ALSO *84) 1938: Salvador Dali sketches Sigmund Freud.*

～80～

1931: GANDHI MEETS CHARLIE CHAPLIN IN THE EAST END OF LONDON

In 1930, Mohandas Gandhi defied the might of the British Empire by going to the seaside (the Dandi Salt March). At the seashore he made salt, thus publicly breaking the British monopoly on the Indian salt trade (the 'salt law'), which forbade the domestic manufacture of this basic commodity. Gandhi was already a world figure, with millions of people sympathetic to his anti-colonial tactic of non-violent civil disobedience, but the salt protest electrified public opinion round the world.

After a brief imprisonment, Gandhi was unconditionally released in March 1931 (tens of thousands of his followers had also been arrested), and the British government agreed a truce with Gandhi, who sailed to London to attend a conference on India's future.

Thousands flocked to see Gandhi, and every celebrity-hunter in the realm wanted to speak to him. Charlie Chaplin had come to London for the première of his film *City Lights*, and at dinner with Winston Churchill told him of his intention to visit Gandhi (who was completely unaware of Chaplin and had never seen a movie). One noble diner snapped that Gandhi should have been kept in jail. Chaplin responded that if so, another Gandhi would rise to defend India. Churchill – who never liked Gandhi and argued with him at the conference – told Chaplin that such views would make him a good Labour MP.

Chaplin was invited to meet Gandhi, who was receiving visitors at Kingsley Hall, a Christian pacifist centre in the East End (Gandhi wanted to live 'among the poor'; his spartan room can still be viewed today). Chaplin told Gandhi that he was wholly in sympathy with him on Indian independence, but was confused by his 'abhorrence of machinery'. If machinery could make work more efficient and increase leisure time, then people could improve their minds and 'enjoy life', which must be a good thing.

Gandhi smiled and pointed out that machinery had made Indians dependent on the British, so it was now the 'patriotic duty' of Indians to weave their own cloth. Independence would come through shedding 'unnecessary things'; violence and oppression would inevitably self-destruct. Chaplin – like many others before him – realized that Gandhi was not just an airy-fairy idealist, but a shrewd and practical thinker. Chaplin stayed for prayers, and reflected on the 'paradox' of this man who was deeply religious yet 'extremely realistic' at the same time.

What happened next
Gandhi met many other notables on his 1931 visit: several bishops, various lords, his old adversary from his days in South Africa, General Smuts, an East End pearly king and queen, George Bernard Shaw (who told Gandhi 'I am Mahatma Minor'), and the educational reformer Maria Montessori. Chaplin's next film, *Modern Times* (1936), was a satire on modern industrial processes, and some see it as deriving from Gandhi's influence, though Chaplin himself said his inspiration came from a Detroit assembly-line worker's views on the dehumanizing nature of his work.

～81～

1933: GIUSEPPE ZANGARA SHOOTS AT PRESIDENT FRANKLIN ROOSEVELT (BUT HITS THE MAYOR OF CHICAGO)

Assassins need luck (☛ SEE 72), and Giuseppe Zangara was simply very unlucky when he tried to assassinate the newly elected US president Franklin Delano Roosevelt. Zangara was an Italian immigrant bricklayer, and had come to believe that the US president was causing him internal pain (FDR was not the first source of Zangara's misery; the previous president, Herbert Hoover, had been his original intended victim).

When he discovered that Roosevelt was giving a speech in Miami, Zangara joined the crowd watching the end of the parade, and stood on a chair (Zangara was five feet tall) to get Roosevelt into the line of fire. The American public was not aware that Roosevelt was a post-polio paraplegic, and that it was only with great difficulty that he managed to raise himself in the car to respond to the cheering crowd. Just after the car stopped, only yards away from the waiting Zangara, an exhausted Roosevelt slumped back in his seat, saying to a newsreel cameraman: 'I'm sorry, I just can't do it.'

Zangara opened fire and managed to get off five or six shots in the direction of his now out-of-sight target, while struggling with members of the crowd who were grappling with him. The whole episode lasted five seconds. Roosevelt was unhurt, but five others were shot, including Mayor Cermak of Chicago. Cermak subsequently died of his wounds, and the fact that Cermak was a noted enemy of Al Capone led to wild speculation that he had been the intended target all along. Zangara, despite being clearly mad, was sent to the electric chair. His last words were 'Pusha da button', and he is one of the few assassins (or wannabe assassins) to feature in a musical: Sondheim's *Assassins*.

What could have happened next?
After John F Kennedy was assassinated in 1963, his vice-president – the Texan Lyndon B Johnson – proved to be one of the great American reformers. Would Roosevelt's vice-president – the Texan John Garner – have been a similar surprise, if Zangara's luck had held? It does not seem likely: Garner was a full-blown reactionary. Like many vice-presidents, he chafed at his largely ceremonial position, which he described as 'a bucket of warm piss'. He was furious when Roosevelt sought a third term in office, and actually ran unsuccessfully against him in the Democratic primary of 1940. Garner does become president in a 1999 Superman comic, *Superman: War of the Worlds* (after Roosevelt is killed by Martians). In this distinctly unappealing parallel universe, Oswald Mosley is the British PM.

— 82 —

1936: ADOLF HITLER WAVES
TO JESSE OWENS

The story of Jesse Owens is one of the most inspiring in American history. As part of the United States team at the 1936 Berlin Olympics, he braved the hostility of the Nazis to triumph with four gold medals. Hitler refused to shake hands with Owens, and stormed out of the stadium in disgust at the sight of a black man defeating the cream of the Aryan race.

Jesse Owens certainly was an inspiring figure and did indeed win four golds at the Berlin Olympics, but the rest of the preceding paragraph is not true. Yet this version of events has become accepted as fact, and Owens himself eventually gave up trying to correct the record; the mythical version was just too powerful. The myth is disproved by both the contemporary documentary record, and by Owens' own testimony. The images within the official German publications of the event, such as *Olympia 1936*, actually celebrate the multiracial harmony among the athletes. Asians, blacks and whites stand smiling side by side, and there is even a touching photograph of Jesse Owens and the great German athlete Luz Long lying on the grass together, sharing a joke, the very model of warm interracial friendship (and a photograph for which it would be difficult to find many equivalents in the United States of 1936).

Owens later said that Long, in a remarkable gesture of sportsmanship, noticed that Owens technique was faulty, and advised him on how to avoid fouling his leaps in the long jump. Though this story has been doubted, the two athletes obviously liked each other. Owens went on to win the long jump, and the stadium photograph shows Owens saluting with his hand to his head while Long gives a Nazi salute a step below him. They walked off together, arm-in-arm.

Admiration for Owens was widespread in Germany. The Berlin crowd gave him huge ovations, and Leni Riefenstahl – Hitler's favourite director – gave Owens equal godlike status with the white athletes in her documentary, *Olympia* (1938). As for Hitler's attitude to Owens, Owens says: 'When I passed the Chancellor he arose, waved his hand at me, and I waved back at him. I think the writers showed bad taste in criticizing the man of the hour in Germany.'

What happened next
Owens has been criticized for giving conflicting accounts of what happened in Berlin, but this is unfair. He found himself the repository of a powerful myth he did not create, one created, essentially, so that America could be comfortable with itself. It has been quietly forgotten that the American Olympic Association, in a very cowardly fashion, dropped two Jewish sprinters from the contest, as has the fact that when Owens returned home, President Roosevelt refused to meet him, on the grounds that honouring a black man would lose him votes. Roosevelt, not Hitler, snubbed Jesse Owens. As for Luz Long, he was badly wounded in battle in Sicily in 1943, and died in a British hospital.

～ *83* ～

1937: THE DUKE OF WINDSOR MEETS (AND SALUTES) HITLER

Edward, Prince of Wales became King Edward VIII in January 1936. By then, Edward had become a bit better at interacting with his subjects than he used to be (☛ SEE 78). Indeed, the old guard felt there was something too 'modern' about the new king. Betjeman's poem 'Death of King George V', describes Edward, the first British monarch to fly, being observed by 'Old men who never cheated' as he lands 'hatless from the air'. Not wearing a hat was only one of his shocking innovations.

The forebodings were justified. Edward was in love with an American divorcee, Mrs Simpson, and only ruled for 327 days, abdicating in December with the words 'you must believe me when I tell you that I have found it impossible to carry the heavy burden of responsibility and to discharge my duties as King as I would wish to do without the help and support of the woman I love'. In the streets, the children sang: 'Hark, the herald angels sing, / Mrs Simpson's pinched our king.'

The two lovers married in June 1937, and went into exile as the Duke and Duchess of Windsor. They became a real embarrassment to Britain in 1937, by visiting Adolf Hitler in his Berchtesgaden retreat. The Nazi propaganda machine gleefully publicized the visit, which managed to unite most of British opinion – except the far right – in dismay, particularly as the duke enthusiastically gave both 'full' and 'modified' Nazi salutes. The duke's stated intention for visiting Germany – to examine German solutions to unemployment – was regarded as ludicrous by most observers, who also mostly regarded the duke's behaviour as naive, but it is entirely possible that in putting himself forward as a friend of Germany, Edward was also positioning himself as a possible future ally of the Nazis in any conflict with Britain. This was a view held by many in both Germany and Britain, though it seems probable that at the meeting Hitler and the duke did no more than exchange banal pleasantries. The only public comment Hitler seems to have made about the Windsors was that Wallis would have made a 'good queen'. Hitler probably only said this to annoy the British. Rumours of Wallis's infidelities abounded, and even diehard monarchists in Britain blanched at the thought of her becoming queen.

What happened next

World War II happened next, in 1939, and Edward became, for Britain, a potentially major irritant. The duke was known to favour a 'negotiated peace' with Hitler, and was packed off to become governor of the Bahamas in 1940 – a position Churchill thought was sufficiently harmless and distant enough for this loose cannon. After the war he and Wallis settled in Paris, where he died in 1972, followed by Wallis in 1986.

– *84* –

1938: SALVADOR DALI SKETCHES SIGMUND FREUD

The great surrealist painter Dali was obsessed with dreams and their significance; Freud was the great explorer of the unconscious, the man who claimed to have revealed the unconscious drives behind our actions and beliefs, and to have unlocked the inner landscape of the sleeping mind in *The Interpretation of Dreams* (1900), a book Dali studied with close attention in 1925. So although Dali and Freud should possibly have been in touch more often, in fact they met only once, in the unlikely setting of north London, where the Freuds settled after fleeing the Nazi takeover of Vienna in June.

Freud received many visitors in London, though he was probably proudest to receive officials from the Royal Society, who brought the Society's charter for him to sign as he was too ill to travel – an unprecedented gesture of respect for someone who was not the monarch. A stream of writers and celebrities came to visit Freud, including H G Wells (Freud wrote to Wells saying he was now fulfilling his childhood fantasy of becoming an Englishman) and old friends such as Princess Marie Bonaparte and the writer Stefan Zweig, who arranged for Dali to visit Freud. Dali came with his wife Gala and the art collector Edward James, who brought along Dali's painting, *The Metamorphosis of Narcissus*, a work inspired by Freud's study of Leonardo da Vinci.

The meeting was somewhat strained. Dali, who consciously saw Freud as a father figure, thought him a bit 'cold' and was presumably rather in awe of him. Freud, evidently taken aback by Dali's appearance, observed quietly that if Spaniards commonly looked like Dali, it was no wonder they were having a civil war. He also told Dali that he felt the work of the surrealists compared unfavourably with that of the old masters. When looking at great works of the past, he said, one looks for the unconscious, but with surrealist art, one looks for the conscious. He does seem to have been pretty impressed with the Dali painting, however, and later said that although he had previously dismissed surrealists as 'nuts', Dali's visit had made him reconsider.

The meeting also produced a masterpiece. While conversing, Dali was also quickly and quietly sketching Freud, and he subsequently worked up the sketch into a pen-and-ink drawing which is proof in itself of Dali's real talent. Freud was dying of cancer, and he was not shown either the sketch or the finished drawing – Zweig felt it showed the great man's imminent death all too clearly.

What happened next
Freud died in September 1939, after the family had become established at 20 Maresfield Gardens, Primrose Hill, which remained the Freud family home until his daughter Anna's death in 1982. It is now the Freud Museum, and contains Dali's drawing of Freud, and many fascinating artefacts – including the famous 'consulting couch'.

☛ SEE ALSO *79) 1927: The Einsteins visit the Freuds.*

━85━

1939: ABEL MEEROPOL SINGS 'STRANGE FRUIT' TO BILLIE HOLIDAY

B illie Holiday did not write the anti-lynching song 'Strange Fruit', though her authorship is asserted in her 1956 ghostwritten autobiography, *Lady Sings the Blues* (she admitted herself, 'I ain't never read that book').

The original source is a poem by the same name, written by the young Jewish poet and communist Abel Meeropol (who also wrote under the pen name of Lewis Allan, the first names of his still-born children). The poem was inspired by a 1930 photograph of the lynching of two young black men in Indiana. Copies of such photographs from the 1920s and 1930s were very popular in the American south. Lynching was still part of the social fabric of the American south in the early 20th century. 'I wrote "Strange Fruit",' said Meeropol, 'because I hate lynching, and I hate injustice, and I hate the people who perpetuate it.'

Meeropol turned the poem into a song, which quickly became a popular protest song in New York (and was sung at Madison Square Gardens by Laura Duncan), prior to Meeropol turning up in April 1939 at a New York club frequented by Holiday called Cafe Society. This club, founded by another Jewish socialist, Barney Josephson, has been described as a 'milestone' in American racial integration, a brave attempt at creating an environment in which white and black could mix socially.

It was Josephson who introduced the two: Meeropol sang the song for Holiday who, Josephson would later say, seems at first not to have understood 'what the hell the song was about', with its ironic references to 'pastoral' and the 'gallant south'. A few days later, Meeropol returned to the club to hear Holiday sing his masterwork: 'She gave a startling, most dramatic and effective interpretation of the song which could jolt the audience out of its complacency anywhere.' This was exactly his intention, and what the song, in Holiday's rendition, has done to listeners ever since.

What happened next
Released in 1939, 'Strange Fruit' eventually sold over a million copies and became one of the most influential protest songs ever written, thanks to its exceptionally rare combination of potent lyrics, a decent melodic line and a beautiful voice. Meeropol also co-wrote the civil rights anthem 'The House I Live In' in 1943, which was used for a 1945 11-minute movie of the same name, in which Frank Sinatra sings about religious tolerance to (white) children. The effect was somewhat lessened by the removal of a stanza explicitly celebrating racial harmony. The movie's distributor evidently felt that America was not yet ready for such radical stuff. A furious Meeropol had to be escorted from the cinema when he saw what had been done to his song. In 1953, Meeropol and his wife Anne adopted Ethel and Julius Rosenberg's two children after their parents' execution for espionage. Meeropol's part in the American civil rights movement has been largely underplayed in the US, perhaps because it remains too embarrassing to give due credit to a staunch communist.

— 86 —

1940: FRANCO AND HITLER CONFER

Meetings between dictators are seldom joyous occasions for the rest of us, but occasionally such meetings can be unpleasant for the participants, too. Such was the case when, in October 1940, Franco and Hitler had their only meeting, on a train stationed at Hendaye on the Franco-Spanish border.

Hitler had of course given Franco decisive help during the Spanish Civil War, which had ended the previous year. The raid on Guernica by Nazi bombers in 1937 had become (and for many remains) one of the defining events of modern warfare (thanks in part to Picasso's painting commemorating the atrocity). Hitler could thus reasonably feel he was due payback from Franco.

The dictators, naturally enough, both had their own agenda, and each was out for what he could get. Franco had his eye on France's colonial territories in North Africa, which Hitler's ally, Vichy France, would not want to give up.

The meeting was meant to decide how much Franco's fascist Spain would help Hitler's Germany during World War II and it remains a much-debated encounter. It has been argued, for example, that Hitler may not even have really wanted Spain as a full-blown partner. Spain had a large army but was still weak from the Civil War, and if Spain came in on Hitler's side but was then overrun by the Allies, the Nazis would face a strategic nightmare. Hitler may well have believed Spanish neutrality was the best bet for him, and wanted to keep Franco out of the war.

Franco subsequently claimed that he had deliberately kept Spain out of the war despite Hitler's entreaties; but some historians argue that Franco wanted in, as in 1940 Hitler looked like a winner. This is a busy little niche of modern history and the question will likely never be settled. We do know it was a very hard bargaining session, and Hitler later declared that he would rather have three or four teeth pulled than go through another negotiating session with Franco.

What happened next
Unlike Hitler and Franco, the train in which they met still exists, as a museum piece. After the meeting, Franco maintained a cautiously informal neutrality that became less cautious and more pro-Allies as the war progressed. In 1943 he finally declared Spain's full neutrality, a blatant display of realpolitik. When the war ended, and as the Cold War progressed, Franco eventually found acceptance from the US in exchange for military bases. His dispatch of volunteers – the 'Blue' division – to join in the Nazi invasion of Russia in 1941 did him no harm in some post-war quarters (the volunteers were recalled to Spain in 1943). One thing should be said for Franco: he was prepared to protect Sephardic Jews (descendants of the Jews expelled from Spain in 1492) throughout Nazi-occupied Europe. A Spanish passport meant protection in Europe throughout the war, and Franco's policy may have saved the lives of tens of thousands of Jewish refugees.

~87~

1945: L RON HUBBARD POSSIBLY MEETS ALEISTER CROWLEY

Religions are often associated with deserts, and Los Angeles, seen by many as a sort of urban wilderness ('there is no there, there', said Gertrude Stein of the city), has witnessed the creation of many cults, or religions in embryo. By the mid-1940s, the notorious British devotee of the Arts of Magic, Aleister Crowley, had mystic communities in many places, including Los Angeles where his devotees included the rocket scientist Jack Parsons, who, it is said, would invoke the god Pan before rocket launches.

Most commentators regard Crowley as an absurd charlatan who used a load of mumbo-jumbo to exploit his vulnerable followers; others went further in their criticism. Crowley's own mother called him 'The Beast', a title he happily adopted, along with the description of him in the British tabloid press as 'the wickedest man in the world' (rumours about Crowley's awful practices abounded, and some of them were even true).

Sometime after World War II ended, Parsons the rocketeer introduced a young science fiction writer called Ron Hubbard to the LA satanic community. Hubbard would later become as controversial a figure in his own way as Crowley, and some sources confidently assert that they definitely met once (Hubbard himself later described Crowley as a friend). However, others regard such a meeting as improbable. At any rate, in early 1946 Parsons wrote to Crowley, telling him about this wonderful convert to necromancy called Ron who had moved in with him. Parsons reported that he planned to incarnate 'a Moonchild' with Hubbard's help. Crowley responded with this rather dubious tribute: 'I thought I had the most morbid imagination but it seems I have not. I cannot form the slightest idea what you can possibly mean.'

What it meant for Parsons soon became clear – in April 1946 Hubbard ran off with Parsons's girlfriend Betty, putting a definitive end to the moonchild project. Adherents of Scientology, the religion Hubbard later founded, have described Hubbard's venture into Crowley's weird world as a rescue mission (Betty became Hubbard's second wife). Crowley wrote to Parsons telling him he had been conned.

What happened next

Parsons blew himself up in his lab in 1952. Hubbard officially founded the Church of Scientology in 1953. Hubbard's son later claimed that his father told him that Scientology came into being on the day Crowley died (in 1947), and it is often asserted that Hubbard derived some inspiration from Crowley's occult system. Crowley is said to be the source for the magician in the M R James story, 'Casting the Runes', but he is probably best known today for his appearance on the cover of the *Sergeant Pepper* album. The Beatles are not the only rock musicians with Crowley connections. Led Zeppelin's Jimmy Page once owned Boleskine House, Crowley's sometime home beside Loch Ness. Claims that the magic rites practised there by the 'Beast' Crowley were responsible for the reappearance of the 'Monster' Nessie should perhaps be left by the rest of us for specialists in the field of metaphysical cryptozoology.

MODERN TIMES
(20th CENTURY
from 1946)

─ 88 ─

1946: WITTGENSTEIN WAVES A POKER IN THE PRESENCE OF KARL POPPER

Philosophy belongs to the world of ideas, and is not commonly pursued with the aid of blunt instruments. However, on a famous occasion, one philosopher (allegedly) laid hands on a poker to make his point.

Ludwig Wittgenstein was one of the greatest 20th-century philosophers, and was almost certainly the only one who knew how to work a howitzer, having served in the Austrian artillery in World War I (he was decorated for bravery). Karl Popper was 13 years younger than Wittgenstein, but like him was from a Jewish Viennese family, was a product of the culture of the declining Austro-Hungarian Empire, and was also a renowned philosopher. Popper's *The Open Society and its Enemies*, a strong defence of the virtues of western liberal democracy, had just been published in 1945.

Yet they had never met before their encounter at the Cambridge Moral Science Club on 25 October, 1946 – and they were never to meet again. The club was a venue where college dons and students could meet to discuss philosophy. On this night the heavyweights were out in force to hear Popper, the guest speaker, give a paper entitled 'Are There Philosophical Problems?'. The club's chairman, Wittgenstein, was present, as was Bertrand Russell. Popper spoke for about ten minutes, and Wittgenstein left when Popper finished. A rumour quickly spread that the two men had duelled with pokers. Popper stated in his 1974 autobiography that Wittgenstein had indeed been waving a poker, making emphatic gestures with it, while asking Popper for an example of a 'moral rule'. Popper says he suggested that a good rule would be 'not to threaten visiting lecturers with pokers', whereupon Wittgenstein threw down the poker and stormed out of the room. Poker apart, the philosophical disagreement between Wittgenstein and Popper was fundamental. For Wittgenstein, philosophy was about the nature of language; the so-called 'problems' of philosophy were simply to do with misuse of language. For Popper, philosophy was about morality, life and how we live together.

What happened next
Wittgenstein died in 1951, but had already challenged Popper's widely circulated version of the poker evening. It seems quite possible that Wittgenstein did wave a poker (academics in full flow often employ props), but it is unlikely he did this in a threatening manner. As for leaving early, he was easily bored and often left meetings early. Several differing versions of the poker incident have been given by some of the other philosophers present, and a partisan element may have influenced the accounts (indeed even the memories) of the more committed disciples of each man. This doesn't say much for the reliability of personal testimony, let alone the quest for truth (one of the supposed aims of philosophy).

Wittgenstein may have had another odd connection with Popper. Wittgenstein went to the same school as Hitler in Linz in 1903-04 (there has been some speculation that he is the 'Jewish boy' remembered with hatred in *Mein Kampf*), and it has been suggested that Hitler – while a struggling artist – may have benefited from a charity supported by Popper's father.

–89–

1946: BERYL FORMBY TELLS DANIEL MALAN TO PISS OFF

The Lancashire-born singer/comedian George Formby was a performer of some genius, whose mixture of ukulele-playing with double entendres may be an acquired taste, but is one many have in fact acquired. George was one of the few English comics always welcome in Scottish music halls.

In 1946, George and his wife/manager Beryl (a former champion clog dancer) flew to South Africa, and Beryl as always demanded the best of everything. The tour organizers were not too familiar with Formby's act and billed him as 'the male Gracie Fields' (still, over 20,000 fans greeted them in Cape Town). The head of the National Party, Daniel Malan (who two years later would introduce apartheid), sent the Formbys a note telling them not to perform to coloured audiences. Beryl – not a woman to order about – ripped up the note and the Formbys decided to perform for black audiences for free. This was quite a statement, as both Beryl and George were tight with their money.

At one show a black child came on stage and gave Beryl a box of chocolates. Beryl picked her up and kissed her, then passed her to George, who did the same, causing an immediate sensation. Next day, Malan sent a delegation to give the Formbys a 'final warning', and of course Beryl slammed the door in their faces. So Malan phoned Beryl and began to berate her. Beryl, at her most magnificent, simply said 'Why don't you piss off, you horrible little man?' and hung up. The Formbys were thrown out of South Africa.

They visited again in 1955 (Malan had meanwhile served as prime minister 1948-54) and defied death threats to again perform before black audiences for free. The South African government was incensed, but there was little they could do but fume. The Formbys had fought the regime to a standstill.

What happened next
From the inception of apartheid in 1948 to its abolition in 1991, the South African government drew much comfort from the visits of entertainers who were prepared to play to segregated audiences. George and Beryl demonstrated that it was possible to challenge apartheid, though few other performers followed their example – Dusty Springfield being one notable exception. The furious reactions of Malan and the National Party leadership to the Formbys' open defiance shows how important such gestures could be, and not just in South Africa. Similarly, in 1955 Marilyn Monroe made a significant breach in the wall of racial discrimination in the US when she persuaded the owner of Hollywood's Mocambo nightclub to allow Ella Fitzgerald to perform on stage – by promising to take a front table for herself every night. In 1955, this was still a brave thing for a white American woman to do; but Monroe, like the Formbys, had a moral backbone.

～90～

1948: MARY MCCARTHY REPRIMANDS LILLIAN HELLMAN

One of the longest-running and most famous literary feuds of the last century was between two writers who met only once, but who, like battleships, fired salvos at each other from a distance for decades – out of sight but within range.

The dramatist Lillian Hellman was born in New Orleans in 1907, and wrote several fine plays, such as *The Children's Hour* (1934), possibly the first Broadway play to tackle lesbianism, and *The Little Foxes* (1939). The novelist Mary McCarthy was born in Seattle in 1912, and is now best known for *The Group* (1963), a novel about the ambitions and sex lives of a group of Vassar graduates. Both women were politically active and joined in many of the leftist campaigns of the 1930s, and although they may have been in the same room together at different points, their 1948 encounter is the only certain face-to-face meeting.

The poet Stephen Spender was teaching literature at Sarah Lawrence College in New York, and asked his (all female) students which women writers they would like to meet. They nominated McCarthy and Hellman, and both accepted Spender's invitation to meet the students. McCarthy arrived late, and stood at the back of the room (she said, perhaps optimistically, that Hellman mistook her for a student). She was in time to hear Hellman tell the students that the novelist John Dos Passos had only made a short visit to Spain in 1937 during the Spanish Civil War, and abandoned the Loyalist (socialist) cause because he didn't like Spanish food. McCarthy was incensed. She later wrote that Hellman was trying to brainwash the students, and described the comment on Dos Passos as 'vicious'. She broke in and told the students: 'I'll tell you why he broke with the Loyalists, you'll find it in his novel, *The Adventures of a Young Man*, and it wasn't such a clean break.' The Dos Passos novel, detailing the progress of a young idealist disillusioned with communism, reflects the experiences of many contemporary socialists, such as

McCarthy herself and George Orwell. McCarthy says Hellman began to 'tremble... it was a very dramatic moment of someone being caught red-handed'.

What happened next
Whatever her other faults may have been, Hellman gave a magnificent response to the House Un-American Activities Committee in 1952 when she was asked to 'name names' of fellow leftists: 'I cannot and will not cut my conscience to fit this year's fashions.' But it was not just McCarthy who accused her of being less than truthful: Muriel Gardiner, who is widely believed to be the original for the writer's friend 'Julia' in Hellman's 1973 memoir *Pentimento*, said she had never even met Hellman. The feud with McCarthy became world news when, in a 1980 TV interview, McCarthy said of Hellman: 'every word she writes is a lie, including "and" and "the"'. Hellman responded with a lawsuit for libel, but died in 1984 before the case came to court. The feud is the subject of Nora Ephron's musical play *Imaginary Friends* (2002).

⁓ *91* ⁓

1956: ERIC NEWBY BUMPS INTO WILFRED THESIGER IN AFGHANISTAN

In early 1956, Eric Newby was working in the fashion industry, trying to sell a poorly designed dress to sceptical buyers ('it was not only a hideous dress; it was soaking up money like a sponge'). Newby, a decorated veteran of both the Black Watch and the Special Boat Squadron, enjoyed the fashion business, but decided to accept ten years of advice to quit and resigned. He then sent a telegram to his diplomat friend Hugh Carless, 'CAN YOU TRAVEL NURISTAN JUNE?'

Until the 1890s, Nuristan, that part of Afghanistan enclosed by the Hindu Kush ('Hindu Killer') mountains, was called Kafiristan: 'Land of the Unbelievers'. The region was little known to outsiders, and had changed little since Kipling used the place for the setting of his short story, 'The Man Who Would be King'. Carless said yes, and discovering that neither knew how to climb, they went to Wales to practise; luckily the waitresses at their inn were experienced climbers and taught them the rudiments.

The expedition was actually quite dangerous. The highest peaks of the Hindu Kush are over 20,000 feet high, and the locals were possibly even more of a threat. After a harrowing time on the mountains, they headed for Kabul by descending into the Lower Panjshir, where the two amateurs ran into the genuine article, the great explorer Wilfred Thesiger. Thesiger was then 46, and Newby's description of the man sums him up as a 'throwback to the Victorian era, a fluent speaker of Arabic, a very brave man, who … apart from a few weeks every year, has passed his entire life among primitive peoples'. In the 1930s, Thesiger had crossed the Arabian Empty Quarter twice, and was the first European to traverse the hostile Danakil country in Abyssinia. During World War II, he had led SAS raids behind German lines in North Africa.

In exploring terms, Thesiger belongs, as Newby said, to an older, imperialist school, a hard world in which shooting lions, crocodiles and bandits was normal, whereas Newby is among the first and certainly one of the finest (and funniest) of the modern, ironic school of travel writer. Yet Thesiger would have rejected Newby's use of the term 'primitive peoples'. For Thesiger, far from being 'primitive', these were the best of people, for whom generosity, simplicity, and courage were everyday virtues. Thesiger told his new companions about the medical treatments he dispensed on his travels, which included surgery, such as 'hundreds' of finger amputations, and, just a few days previously, an eye removal. The exhausted Newby and Carless began pumping up their airbeds on the 'iron' ground. 'God,' said Thesiger, 'you must be a couple of pansies.'

What happened next
Newby's account of working as a seaman in 1938 on the last merchant sailing voyage between Britain and Australia, *The Last Grain Race*, was to be published later in 1956, establishing him immediately as a travel writer of note. Thesiger's 'couple of pansies' gibe is the last line in Newby's account of the Nuristan adventure, *A Short Walk in the Hindu Kush* (1958), which includes Thesiger's photograph of the

two 'failures', Newby and Carless. Thesiger died in 2003, Newby in 2006.

~92~

1958: LUIS BUÑUEL ASKS ALEC GUINNESS TO BE HIS LEAD ACTOR

Of the many 'might have been' movies in the history of cinema, one of the most intriguing is the movie the great Spanish director Luis Buñuel wanted to make of Evelyn Waugh's dark little satire on the Los Angeles funeral business, *The Loved One* (1948), with one of England's greatest actors, Alec Guinness, in the lead role. This movie would surely have been different from the surrealist gem Buñuel made with Salvador Dali, *Un chien andalou* (1929), but it would certainly have been a very interesting film.

Guinness and Waugh had met in 1956 at Edith Sitwell's reception into the Roman Catholic Church (both men were themselves converts). They took to each other, and the notoriously bad-tempered Waugh later wrote to a friend 'I liked Alec Guinness so much'. A few years later, before leaving to attend a film festival in Mexico, Guinness received a filmscript based on Waugh's novel. The script had been partly written by Buñuel, and when Guinness arrived in Mexico City the Spaniard visited him to discuss the project. Buñuel began their meeting by telling Guinness that he had asked some critics how they liked the music in his last film. They had responded that it was 'wonderful.' 'I promise', Buñuel said to Guinness, 'there is not one note of music in the movie.' Guinness had a similar impish sense of humour, and described Buñuel's film ideas about *The Loved One* as 'very simple, true to the novel and yet sometimes daringly odd ... We got on well and I was thrilled at the prospect of working with him.'

Alas, the film was never made, possibly, as Guinness believed, because the film rights were not acquired in time. Instead, Tony Richardson directed a version which appeared in 1965, and which few Waugh aficionados like. It was as far removed, thought

Guinness, 'from the factual, debunking spirit of Waugh as a flying saucer'.

What happened next
Buñuel and Guinness never worked together, which is a loss to cinema. There was an affinity between them, as religion was deeply important to both, though in rather different ways (Buñuel observed that he was 'an atheist, thank God'). Waugh wrote to a friend, after Edith Sitwell's reception, 'I know I am awful. But how much more awful I should be without the faith', a comment that Guinness's biographer Piers Paul Read says could perhaps also be made of Guinness.

☛ SEE ALSO *97) 1978: Alec Guinness has lunch with 'M'.*

～93～
1960: FIDEL CASTRO WINS THE ERNEST HEMINGWAY PRIZE

In 1960, the tenth annual International Marlin Fishing Tournament earned a place in history by being a rare example of a national sporting competition being won by the head of the country, the prime minister, Fidel Castro.

The marlin competition had been founded in 1950 by Ernest Hemingway, who had moved to Cuba from Key West in 1939, and, as Michael Palin has observed, was 'never really happy with any activity unless some sort of contest was involved'. Marlin fishing was one of his passions, and not long after founding the contest he wrote his novel about an old Cuban fisherman's struggle to catch a huge marlin – *The Old Man and the Sea* (1952). In the novel (there is a fine movie version starring Spencer Tracy and a big fish) the old fisherman, Santiago, straps the marlin to the side of the boat and heads back for home, fighting off sharks who eventually strip the marlin to the bone. The fish would have sold for a lot in the market, but Santiago thinks no one is worthy of eating it anyway. The duel between the man and the marlin is what matters, not the fish's market value.

In 1960 the tournament was named after Hemingway, a decision he was not entirely happy about. He called the renaming 'a lousy posthumous tribute to a lousy living writer'. Even some great admirers of his work had suggested that the post-war Hemingway was in danger of becoming self-parodic – what Hemingway saw as correct male behaviour was increasingly seen as macho posturing – and Hemingway's response to the renaming suggests he may not have been unaware of the danger that his talents were fading.

Castro loved fishing too, and was delighted to be the worthy winner of the competition, and the fact that it was now named after Hemingway undoubtedly added flavour to the victory. He regarded the American as an inspirational figure, and described Hemingway's novel about the Spanish Civil War, *For Whom the Bell Tolls* (1940), as a key influence on the Cuban revolutionary struggle.

There are several photographs of the prize-giving at the end of the tournament, and one particularly good one by the revolutionary photographer Osvaldo Sales, showing, as Hemingway's niece Hilary said, the 'two most famous beards' of the age together at last. The event concluded with Hemingway presenting Castro with the winner's cup. It was the only time the two met, and it is said they exchanged 'pleasantries'. Hemingway, in truth, was not that sympathetic to the Cuban Revolution, but refrained from criticizing Castro in public, which he would have regarded as ungentlemanly, if not unmanly, behaviour.

What happened next
Hemingway left Cuba in 1960, settled in Idaho, and shot himself in 1961. Castro went on to become one of the world's longest-serving heads of state, but seems to have won no more fishing competitions. Marlin are still fished for by tourists to Cuba, but they are nowadays tagged and released instead of being killed.

— 94 —

1963: JOSEPHINE BAKER STANDS BESIDE MARTIN LUTHER KING

Josephine Baker, one of the world's most famous, popular and influential dancers, was also a war heroine with a life worthy of Hollywood – but being black, she was pretty much unknown in the US, her country of birth, until the 1950s. She was born in St Louis in 1906, and became a vaudeville performer in her teens, then travelled to Paris in 1925 as a member of *La Revue Nègre*. African-American jazz was all the rage in 1920s Paris, and Baker quickly established herself as a popular performer on the cabaret scene.

African art of all kinds was prized for its sensuality; Baker's stage performances as a dancer added wit, humour and simple clowning to the mix. She was beautiful, clever, talented, made people laugh, and sometimes wore a skirt made of bananas. Paris loved her, and she soon opened her own club – Chez Josephine. In 1927 she also starred in a movie, *La Sirène des Tropiques* (a poor film, but it does show her dancing in her prime – early film of Baker can also usually be found on YouTube).

During World War II Baker worked as an agent for French military intelligence and in 1946 was awarded the *Rosette de la Résistance* and became a knight of the *Légion d'honneur*. Baker retired in the mid-1950s to look after her twelve adopted children, her 'rainbow tribe' (her only natural child was stillborn in 1941), and fell upon hard times. She resolutely refused to perform before segregated audiences, even though she desperately needed the money (Princess Grace of Monaco was among the benefactors who rallied to Baker's support).

In 1963, Baker joined the 'March on Washington for Jobs and Freedom' and was invited onto the platform. She was wearing her Free French uniform and her *Légion d'honneur* medal. Other prominent black female entertainers on the march included Eartha Kitt, Lena Horne, and Mahalia Jackson, though Baker was the only woman – white or black – given a chance to speak by the male organizers. She gave a 'Tribute to Women', introducing Rosa Parks and other 'Negro Women Fighters for Freedom' to the crowd, which she charmed, as she had done throughout her career. Standing proudly next to Martin Luther King, she told the multiracial crowd it was 'salt and pepper – just what it should be'. No one that day put it better.

What happened next
As had happened with Lincoln's legendary Gettysburg Address in 1863, the American newspapers largely failed to see – despite the proximity of the Lincoln Memorial – the significance of the march, and made little mention of any of the speeches, even King's speech. And while King's speech is now remembered for the 'I have a dream' segment, he, like the other speakers, was actually talking hardball for most of the time: 'There will be neither rest nor tranquillity in America until the Negro is granted his citizenship.' Baker died of a stroke in 1975, and was given a state funeral in Paris.

～95～

1963: BILL CLINTON SHAKES PRESIDENT JOHN F KENNEDY'S HAND

In July 1963 the 16-year-old Bill Clinton went to Washington as a delegate for Boys Nation, a civic training organization set up by the American Legion. Each delegate received a handshake from the president, and archive film and photographs show Kennedy and the young Clinton shaking hands and beaming at each other. Clinton's presidential ambitions are generally said to date from that handshake (the other great influence on the young Clinton was Martin Luther King, whose 'I have a dream' speech he memorized).

Kennedy had just returned from a trip to Europe, and mentioned this in the speech he gave to the boys in the White House Rose Garden. Addressing them as 'Gentlemen', he said he was impressed in Europe 'by the strong feeling that most people have, even though they may on occasions be critical of our policies; a strong feeling that the United States stands for freedom, that the promises in the Constitution and the Declaration of Independence while they may not be fully achieved we are attempting to move to the best of our ability in that direction, that without the United States they would not be free and with the United States they are free, and it is the United States which stands on guard all the way from Berlin to Saigon'.

Ronald Reagan's later presidential declaration that America was a 'shining city on a hill' has been much mocked, but – allowing for Kennedy's qualification that American aspirations 'may not be fully achieved' – Reagan's vision does not differ in essentials from the sentiments expressed in the earlier president's speech.

What happened next
Less than six years after the meeting in the Rose Garden, Clinton was a Rhodes scholar at Oxford University, and campaigning against the Vietnam War that Kennedy had taken a major role in starting. The jury is still considering its verdict on Clinton's presidency, but Kennedy's reputation has been in steep decline on many fronts in recent years, from foreign policy to personal morality. If things continue like this, he may even be popularly remembered not as a heroic and inspirational young president, but mainly as the source for the decidedly uninspirational Mayor Quimby in *The Simpsons*.

—96—

1965: ELVIS PRESLEY JAMS WITH THE BEATLES

There have been many encounters between famous musicians that no one could have recorded. Maddeningly, it would have been perfectly possible to make a recording when the Beatles met Elvis, but no one bothered. In 1965 the Beatles were touring America for the second time and visited Elvis at his Bel Air house. There had been some attempts in the press to present the two acts as rivals – America versus Britain and so forth – but in fact the Beatles thought Elvis was magnificent, and Elvis, publicly at least, returned the admiration. Indeed, in 1964, just before their electrifying appearance on the *Ed Sullivan Show*, Sullivan read out – to about 70 million viewers – a telegram from Elvis praising the Beatles.

The Beatles had tried to meet Elvis on their first US tour in 1964 but Elvis's manager, Colonel Parker, who probably felt the upstart Brits should know their place, apparently sent them a few Elvis souvenirs, and that was it. According to Priscilla Presley's account in *Elvis by the Presleys* (2005), when John, Paul, George and Ringo walked into the room, Elvis remained reclining on the sofa watching the TV with the sound off. Elvis 'rarely got up', says Priscilla. The Beatles maintained a respectful silence, expecting the 'King' to set the ball rolling. After this subdued start, Elvis put a record on – possibly Charlie Rich – and played along with a bass guitar (he had been teaching himself bass, McCartney was surprised to learn). The Beatles got hold of a few guitars and began jamming with Elvis. There was, says Priscilla, more music than talk – the Beatles were shy, and Elvis was not disposed to talk much – but the music was 'sweet', she adds. Sadly, no one took any pictures, let alone recorded anything. At the end, the Beatles invited Elvis to visit them at their leased house – Elvis smiled and said 'We'll see', but, adds Priscilla, 'I knew he had no intention of returning the visit. Elvis rarely went out in Hollywood'.

What happened next
Just five years later, in December 1970, Elvis sent a handwritten note to the White House asking to meet President Nixon and, being the King, was granted an audience. Presley still looked like a rock-and-roll hero, but his career had already started to descend into the freak-show act he would shortly become. Elvis gave Nixon a gift of a pistol, and launched into a tirade about how British entertainers, particularly the Beatles, were anti-American and spreading drug culture. Elvis asked the president for a Bureau of Narcotics and Dangerous Drugs badge, and was later sent an honorary one, which he seems to have thought meant he had legal powers. It is now on display at Graceland, Elvis's home. Elvis died in 1977, his health ruined by junk food and substance abuse.

~97~

1978: ALEC GUINNESS HAS LUNCH WITH 'M'

By August 1978, Alec Guinness had long been a grand old man of the stage, but had also acquired a new, huge (and unwanted) fan base for playing Ben Obi-Wan Kenobi in *Star Wars* (1977). Guinness says that Harrison Ford referred to him as the 'Mother Superior', which was perhaps affectionately meant, as Ford and Guinness shared a distaste for the unspeakable (in every sense) script (Ford famously said to director George Lucas: 'George, you can write this shit, but you can't say it').

Guinness wanted to put *Star Wars* behind him, so when he was offered the part of George Smiley in a BBC TV adaptation of John Le Carré's novel *Tinker, Tailor, Soldier, Spy* (1974), he accepted. Le Carré had in fact made it plain to the BBC that he believed only Alec Guinness could play the enigmatic Smiley. Guinness took the role despite misgivings about the 'passive' nature of Smiley, so Le Carré arranged to host a lunch for Guinness and the former head of MI6, Sir Maurice Oldfield, who was claimed by some to be the model for both Smiley (Le Carré denies this) and 'M' in the James Bond films.

Le Carré described Guinness and Oldfield as 'cuddling up and I was an intrusion'. Guinness assumed that Oldfield was the raw material for Smiley, and studied the former spy chief closely: 'Liked him. A bit plumper and shorter than me ... execrable tie, tatty shirt, good suit, flashy cufflinks and bright orange shoes.' Le Carré recalled: 'At the end of the lunch, Oldfield left and Guinness watched him go down the road ... He then says, "Do they all wear those very vulgar cufflinks?"'

Guinness's characterization of Smiley, which emerged from the meeting, ended up a blend of elements from both Oldfield (including the orange shoes and cufflinks) and Le Carré. Oldfield was an admirer of Guinness but why he agreed to the lunch – knowing Guinness would be studying him – is unclear.

What happened next

After the TV spy saga, Guinness returned to the (lucrative) grind of the *Star Wars* sequels, partly because of gratitude for Lucas's gift of a post-contract increase in royalties. Oldfield – who died in 1981 – got what he may well have wished for, a dignified, intelligent portrayal of a civilized British spy chief. But how realistic a picture does it give of the British Secret Service? At least one agent – Malcolm Muggeridge – wondered if the weird outfit he had joined was a parallel organization, set up to protect the real Secret Service. It is clear from Muggeridge's and similar memoirs that there was no golden 'James Bond' era for British espionage. Guinness's earlier role as the hapless Hoover salesman turned spy in the 1959 movie *Our Man in Havana* – based on a novel written by another British agent, Graham Greene – may well have been closer to the mark than the archly sophisticated spook he later played.

☛ SEE ALSO *92) 1958: Luis Buñuel asks Alec Guinness to be his lead actor.*

～98～

1985: JACKIE KENNEDY POPS DOWNSTAIRS TO MEET PRINCESS DIANA

Princess Diana and Jacqueline Kennedy Onassis had much in common. Their parents went through bitter divorces, they each had what could be regarded as 'arranged' marriages to men over a decade older than they were, and they lived their married lives in the glare of public and press scrutiny. They were popular with the general public, both men and women, who followed their lives in the press. Both were leaders of fashion, but also used fashion as a form of protective armour (Jackie's words to a designer: 'Protect me – I am so mercilessly exposed and I don't know how to cope with it', could apply to them both). And while the family into which Diana married was the supposedly ancient British royal family, the Windsor dynasty is not actually that much older than the Kennedys.

In 1985, Diana and Prince Charles travelled to Washington DC to open a show celebrating centuries of British upper-class art patronage. The American socialite Bunny Mellon invited the royal couple to her Virginia estate to meet some young blood (which was perhaps not absolutely blue, but was certainly well-connected). Among them were John F Kennedy Jr and Caroline Kennedy. Their mother, Jackie Kennedy, who was upstairs, left her children and Diana to chat for a while, before popping downstairs to join in. It was to be the only time these two iconic figures ever met. It would be nice to know what they chatted about, but those who were there are not telling. We do know, however, that Diana admired Jackie, and Jackie, at least to begin with, admired Diana, though she later described her as having 'disembowelled herself in public'.

The Kennedy biographer Jay Mulvaney points out that whereas Jackie adopted a British stiff-upper-lip approach to the difficulties posed by President Kennedy's infidelities, Diana went in for American-style, tell-all self-revelation through the media. Arguably, however, nothing in Diana's love life was ever comparable to the shock in Ireland at Jackie's marriage to Onassis in 1968, when grown women wept in the streets at this supposed betrayal of the Kennedy legend.

What happened next
Diana wept when Jackie died in 1994, and wrote a letter of condolence to Caroline and John in which she described their mother as a 'role model' for bringing up children in public. Caroline Kennedy and Diana had a macabre connection of their own: in 1975, Caroline, then 17, came close to being killed by an IRA bomb intended for Sir Hugh and Lady Antonia Fraser, with whom she was staying, while in 1983 there was an IRA plan to murder Charles and Diana with a bomb while they attended a concert at a London theatre.

～99～

1985: KURT WALDHEIM PUNCHES JOHN SIMPSON

In 1972, the respected Austrian statesman Kurt Waldheim succeeded U Thant as Secretary-General of the United Nations, a post he held for two terms, until 1981. He tried to stand for a third term, but his attempt was vetoed by China.

In 1985, Waldheim began campaigning for the Austrian presidency, and also published his memoir *In the Eye of the Storm*. The memoir concentrated on his UN role, and this prompted several journalists to begin asking questions about Waldheim's role in World War II, particularly his time as an intelligence officer in the Balkans, when ferocious reprisals were being carried out against Yugoslav civilians, prisoners were being tortured and executed, and trains and trucks bore victims to death camps. When challenged about his role in all this, Waldheim took the line that he had been a simple soldier carrying out clerical duties, and knew nothing of any of the horrors taking place – which, as has been said, made Waldheim the worst-informed military intelligence officer in history.

The presidential campaign in Austria thus attracted a lot of international attention, and observers noted how Waldheim was being rapturously cheered by veterans of Hitler's war wherever he went. John Simpson of the BBC went to one such emotionally charged election meeting, described in his enthralling autobiography, *A Mad World, My Masters* (2000). Simpson asked Waldheim if he was going to win. Waldheim replied, yes, and said the people loved him, as Simpson could see. Simpson then asked a rather direct question: 'Even though in today's British press there are accusations that you ordered the execution of several British prisoners of war?'

Waldheim seems to have punched Simpson in the stomach even before he finished asking the question. Simpson had been punched in the stomach before by a politician, in 1970, by the then British prime minister Harold Wilson, and Simpson says Wilson's punch was harder (it floored him, in fact). Waldheim's assault on Simpson was filmed by an American camera team and caused a sensation in Austria. Nevertheless, Waldheim was elected president in 1986.

What happened next
Also in 1986, Waldheim gave one of the oddest wedding gifts in history to Arnold Schwarzenegger (who held dual Austrian and American citizenship) when he married Maria Shriver. Waldheim was invited to the wedding, but wisely did not attend, and sent instead a life-size papier-mâché statue of Schwarzenegger, clad in lederhosen, carrying off Shriver clad in a dirndl. Someone who saw this strange object described it as 'sinister', but Andy Warhol's diary records Schwarzenegger's delighted reaction to the gift. Waldheim served as Austrian president until 1992. In 1994 the US Justice Department concluded that Waldheim had indeed been guilty of war crimes and barred him from the US. A few months later, Pope John Paul II gave Waldheim a papal knighthood.

~100~

2000: SAMI AL-ARIAN PROMISES TO SUPPORT GEORGE W BUSH

When a group of hopefuls seeking the Republican candidacy for the presidency were asked in December 1999, 'What political philosopher or thinker do you most identify with and why?', Governor Bush responded 'Christ, because he changed my heart'. Bush had become a born-again Christian in the mid-1980s.

In March 2000, George Bush visited the key state of Florida during his campaign to become the Republican candidate for the US presidency. Florida is a state with a large Muslim population, and Bush was an active seeker of Muslim votes. Most Christians – such as Bush – regard Christ as part of the godhead, the Trinity. Muslims regard Christ as a prophet, but not divine. Republican campaigners in 2000 did not, however, dwell on theological differences, but rather on the American 'centre-right' social values they claimed Republicans shared with Muslims: pro-family, anti-